# ENCHANTED APRIL

### BY **MATTHEW BARBER**

**FROM THE NOVEL BY
ELIZABETH VON ARNIM**

★ **Definitive Edition**

★

**DRAMATISTS
PLAY SERVICE
INC.**

ENCHANTED APRIL
Copyright © 1995, 2003, 2004, 2011, Matthew Barber

## SPECIAL NOTE

Anyone receiving permission to produce ENCHANTED APRIL is required to give credit to the Author as sole and exclusive Author of the Play on the title page of all programs distributed in connection with performances of the Play and in all instances in which the title of the Play appears for purposes of advertising, publicizing or otherwise exploiting the Play and/or a production thereof. The name of the Author must appear on a separate line, in which no other name appears, immediately beneath the title and in size of type equal to 50% of the size of the largest, most prominent letter used for the title of the Play. No person, firm or entity may receive credit larger or more prominent than that accorded the Author. Elizabeth von Arnim's name must appear immediately beneath the Author's in size of type no less than 50% of the size of the largest, most prominent letter used for the Author's name. The billing must appear as follows:

ENCHANTED APRIL
by Matthew Barber
from the novel by Elizabeth von Arnim

The following acknowledgments must appear on the title page in all programs distributed in connection with performances of the Play:

Originally produced on Broadway by The Enchanted April Company, LLC.

World premiere February 24, 2000, at Hartford Stage.

In addition, if the music below is used in performances, the following acknowledgment must appear on the title page in all programs in size of type equal to that used for the production designers:

Sound design and original music by John Gromada.

## SPECIAL NOTE ON MUSIC

A CD of the sound design and original music composed for this play by John Gromada is available through the Play Service for $35.00, plus shipping and handling. The nonprofessional fee for the use of this music is $20.00 per performance.

ENCHANTED APRIL was originally produced by the Hartford Stage Company (Michael Wilson, Artistic Director) in Hartford, Connecticut, in February 2000. It was directed by Michael Wilson; the set design was by Tony Straiges; the lighting design was by Rui Rita; the original music and sound design were by John Gromada; the costume design was by Jess Goldstein; and the production stage manager was Wendy Beaton. The cast was as follows:

LOTTY WILTON ................................................. Isabel Keating
MELLERSH WILTON ............................................. John Hines
ROSE ARNOTT ................................................... Enid Graham
FREDERICK ARNOTT .......................... Christopher Donahue
CAROLINE BRAMBLE ................................. Stephanie March
ANTONY WILDING ..................................... Christopher Duva
MRS. GRAVES .......................................................... Jill Tanner
COSTANZA ......................................................... Irma St. Paule


ENCHANTED APRIL opened on Broadway at the Belasco Theatre on April 29, 2003, produced by Jeffrey Richards/Richard Gross/ Ellen Berman, Raymond J. and Pearl Berman Greenwald, Irving Welzer, Libby Adler Mages/Mari Glick, Howard R. Berlin, Terry E. Schnuck and Frederic B. Vogel. It was directed by Michael Wilson; the set design was by Tony Straiges; the lighting design was by Rui Rita; the original music and sound design were by John Gromada; the costume design was by Jess Goldstein; and the production stage manager was Katherine Lee Boyer. The cast was as follows:

LOTTY WILTON ................................................. Jayne Atkinson
MELLERSH WILTON ................................... Michael Cumpsty
ROSE ARNOTT ............................................... Molly Ringwald
FREDERICK ARNOTT ...................................... Daniel Gerroll
CAROLINE BRAMBLE .......................... Dagmara Dominczyk
ANTONY WILDING ..................................... Michael Hayden
MRS. GRAVES .................................................. Elizabeth Ashley
COSTANZA ...................................................... Patricia Conolly

# CHARACTERS

LOTTY WILTON, 30, a Hampstead housewife

MELLERSH WILTON, 32, her husband, a solicitor

ROSE ARNOTT, 40, a Hampstead housewife

FREDERICK ARNOTT, 45, her husband, a writer

CAROLINE BRAMBLE, 25, a socialite

ANTONY WILDING, 25, an artist

MRS. GRAVES, 70s, a London matron

COSTANZA, 60s, an Italian housekeeper


ACT ONE: London, England.

ACT TWO: Genoa, Italy.

TIME: 1922.


# AUTHOR'S NOTE

The two acts of *Enchanted April* are intentionally different from each other in form, crafted to lead the audience on the same sensory journey as the play's characters. Act One should project the heavy, haunted atmosphere of mourning, with each scene blending into the next, the Act gradually building in momentum like a train gaining speed. (The humor will show itself. In fact, the more heavyhearted the overall tone of Act One, the stronger and more bittersweet the humor, and the brighter and more celebratory the rewards of Act Two.)

Scene "changes" in Act One should occur without breaking the Act's flow, consisting of nothing more than swift rearrangements of the four chairs, the taking off and putting on of coats and hats, small lighting changes, and the designated sound cues. Props in each scene should be brought on and off by the actors involved, or by a stagehand costumed as a servant.

# ENCHANTED APRIL

## ACT ONE

### Scene 1

*Darkness. Half-light rises on two tables, four chairs, a coat rack with coats and umbrellas. Rose Arnott sits at one table. Lotty Wilton stands at the other, looking off. Thunder, followed by the sound of steady rain. Lights up in a London ladies' club, 1922. "The Great War" is over by four years, and with it the lives of one million British men. Rose reads a copy of the* London Times. *Lotty gazes out of an unseen window. Both are dressed heavily in dark colors, hair up, with hats on or nearby. Lotty's appearance suggests uncertainty. Rose is spare to the point of severity. Lotty speaks to us. Her essence is of deep sadness and withering valiance, from which genuine hope spontaneously and regularly bursts forth, leaving her endlessly off-balance.*

LOTTY. I was once told the story of a man who, while surveying the grounds of his home, dug his walking stick into the earth, as a reminder of where he wished to one day have an acacia tree. One he could watch from his veranda, and lie under with his wife on warm summer afternoons, cooled in the shadow of its white flowers, and blanketed in their sweet scent. But when planting season came 'round and he returned with a spade and an acacia sapling, the man was vexed. The stick he had left had taken root and begun to grow. It was nearly as tall as himself now, in fact, with young, awkward branches and small clusters of frail new leaves. This, on the very spot that was to be his acacia. The man buried his spade into the ground to unearth the strange thing ... but stopped. For among the leaves, underneath, he spied a small blossom.

*(Enchanted.)* It was acacia. *(Considers.)* "Enchantment," some would say. Or "providence," perhaps. I suppose the only real certainty is that the fellow had lost a perfectly good walking stick. If that's the part you choose to see. The rest is open to opinion. *(Sighs, thinks.)* Were it only that some enchantment would step in for us all, to change what we have into what we wish for. To bridge the awkward gap between all of our many befores and afters. Because, for every after found, a before must be lost. And loss is, by nature, an unbalancing thing. More unbalancing, however, is to discover your before gone without an after having taken its place. Leaving you merely to wait and to wonder if there is to be an after at all. Or if, perhaps, waiting and wondering are your after in themselves. *(Thinks.)* I wasn't expecting my after to begin that day at my ladies' club. I wasn't waiting for enchantment to show itself, or providence. I had merely been gazing out of the window, wondering if the rain was ever going to stop. And what my husband might like for dinner that night. And about the fact that the day before I had wondered the same things. And surely would the following day, and the day after that, and the day after. When I came upon the advertisement.

ROSE.  *(Reading.)* "To those who appreciate wisteria and sunshine … "

LOTTY.  A small advert, placed discreetly in the agony column of the *Times*.

ROSE.  "Small castle on the Mediterranean, Northern Italy … "

LOTTY.  Heaven!

ROSE.  "To be let for the month of April. Cook, gardens, ocean view. Reply Box Eleven."

LOTTY.  *(Beaming.)* The words washed over me, filling me suddenly with warmth and peacefulness, as if the advertisement were there especially for me, and was pleased I'd found it. "To those who appreciate wisteria and sunshine." That's me! *(Thunder. Considers.)* But who am I to be reading about Italian castles, and Aprils on the Mediterranean? Who am I? *(Inspired.)* But then, why would I bother to read the newspaper at my ladies' club, when I surely would read my husband's copy tomorrow morning after housekeeping? And why would I come to my club at all on a Tuesday, when my regular city day is Wednesday? And certainly why would I notice the lady, that particular lady I see so often at church, and was thinking of only moments ago? Providence? Enchantment? *(To Rose, with great enthusiasm.)* Are you reading about the castle and the wisteria?

ROSE. *(Invaded.)* I beg your pardon?

LOTTY. *(Breathlessly.)* The advertisement about the castle. It sounds so wonderful, doesn't it? Can you just imagine? Italy and sunshine and wisteria. And when I saw you … you, of all people … well, I couldn't help but think … well, I mean, all this rain … and, oh, the Mediterranean … imagine … and this not even being my city day … well, I … I … *(Suddenly painfully uncomfortable.)* Oh, I am sorry. Here we've only just met and I must apologize already. My husband says that my mind is like a hummingbird. One seldom sees it land. I feel I know you. And yet we've never actually met. My husband and I see you in church in Hampstead.

ROSE. *(Stone-faced.)* I see.

LOTTY. You are our "disappointed Madonna." I see you each Sunday, marshalling in the children from Sunday School, always so right on time for services, and with the schoolchildren so very well-behaved. And I once commented to my husband that you looked to me somewhat like a disappointed Madonna.

ROSE. *(Flummoxed.)* I …

LOTTY. My husband had been speaking to me about finding satisfaction through doing one's job well. Saying something about that if one does one's job well, then one will *not* feel lost, but will instead be automatically bright and brisk with satisfaction. And, seeing you, I just felt that … well, that surely there is also the chance for a certain … disappointment.

ROSE. *(Choosing patience, as she so often must.)* Perhaps it would be best if we begin at the beginning. I am Mrs. Arnott. Rose.

LOTTY. Thank you. I am Lotty. Charlotte. Mrs. Wilton.

ROSE. Right, then.

LOTTY. *(Sadly.)* I don't expect that conveys much to you, "Wilton." Sometimes it doesn't seem to convey anything to me, either. Such a small, sad name. I don't like names.

ROSE. Do you need some kind of advice, Mrs. Wilton?

LOTTY. Oh, no. It was just the advertisement. It sounded so wonderful, that's all.

ROSE. I'm sure it's only this gloomy weather that makes it seem so.

LOTTY. Then you were reading it?

ROSE. *(Caught.)* I … was.

LOTTY. *(Excitedly.)* I knew it! I saw it!

ROSE. Saw it?

LOTTY. The two of us. At the castle.

ROSE. Yourself and your husband.

LOTTY. Oh no, me and you!

ROSE. *(Losing her patience, self-consciously hushed.)* Mrs. Wilton!

LOTTY. Do you ever see things in a kind of a flash before they happen?

ROSE. Never.

LOTTY. Really? Well, when I saw you, I suddenly saw us both, you and me, on the shores of the Mediterranean. Surrounded by beauty. Beauty and blissful peace.

ROSE. Really, Mrs. Wilton. And our husbands? *(Lotty thinks.)*

LOTTY. I didn't see them. I've never seen Mr. Arnott. He is "with us," then?

ROSE. Oh, yes. Quite.

LOTTY. One never knows these days. So many war widows.

ROSE. Sad times.

LOTTY. Perhaps that's why we need something beautiful now. To remind us of the possibility. *(They think.)* I did see us, Rose.

ROSE. Well, that is really most extraordinary, Mrs. Wilton.

LOTTY. Isn't it? Isn't it wonderful enough just to think about? April in Italy. And here it's February already. In two months we could be in it all!

ROSE. It's easy to think of such things, Mrs. Wilton. But it's no use wasting one's time thinking too long.

LOTTY. Oh, but it is! It's essential! And I really do believe, if one considers hard enough, things can happen!

ROSE. I'm not sure I believe that.

LOTTY. *(Becoming increasingly emotional.)* But you must! Even if it isn't true! I've been saving a nest egg, from my dress allowance. It's not much, but my husband himself encouraged me to save it for a rainy day. My husband speaks often of rainy days. My husband speaks often of many things. I could never have imagined spending it on a holiday, but if this isn't that rainy day, well …

ROSE. Money, I fear …

LOTTY. Rose. Close your eyes and think with all of your heart of getting away from Hampstead, from husbands, from this relentless rain, from everything. To heaven!

ROSE. You shouldn't say things like that, Mrs. Wilton.

LOTTY. But it would be heavenly!

ROSE. Heaven isn't somewhere else. It is here and now, within us. We are told that on the very highest authority. The kindred points of heaven and home. Heaven is in our home. *(Lotty considers.)*

LOTTY. But it isn't.

ROSE. But it is. It is there, if we choose, if we make it.

LOTTY. *(Upset, near tears.)* I do choose, and I do make it. And it isn't. I've done nothing but what was expected of me all of my life, and thought that was goodness. I thought I would be ... well ... rewarded in some way, I suppose. That's selfish, I know. But it was what I was told. One prepares, is good, and is rewarded. I didn't know how quickly things change. That one must keep an eye on what one is preparing for, in case it no longer even exists. Someone forgot to tell me that. Where everyone is racing to, I don't know. I only know that I've been left behind. No. Now I'm convinced that there are blind sorts of goodness and there are ... enlightened sorts of goodness. Women such as ourselves have been living the blind sort. Preparing for nothing but ... oblivion.

ROSE. *(Hardening, scowling.)* Mrs. Wilton. I assure you that I am a most happy individual.

LOTTY. *(Defeated.)* Yes. Of course. Will you believe that I have never in my life spoken like this to anyone?

ROSE. It's the weather, I'm sure.

LOTTY. *(Adrift.)* Yes. And the advertisement.

ROSE. Yes.

LOTTY. And both of us being so miserable. *(Sadly.)* Something has been lost, Rose. Something has shifted, and I don't recognize anything anymore.

ROSE. *(Moved.)* We must all deal with loss, Mrs. Wilton. Each in his way.

LOTTY. Yes. That's true. But don't you ever wish you could go back, to hold on tighter? But we can't, can we? We can only go forward. But how? This I haven't seen.

ROSE. Do you see things often, Mrs. Wilton?

LOTTY. Lotty. Yes, I do. But seeing and doing are two different things, aren't they? *(They think.)* "To those who appreciate wisteria and sunshine." *(Lotty smiles wistfully.)* That's you and me, Rose. That much I do see. *(Thunder.)*

# Scene 2

*Rain. The Wilton home. A table, two chairs, a coat rack with coats and umbrellas. Mellersh Wilton sits at the table, looking into a small table mirror, trimming his moustache. A towel is draped around his neck, underneath which he is dressed for an evening business engagement, save for an untied tie. Lotty flutters around him, preparing herself.*

MELLERSH. *(Who believes himself to be the image of premature wisdom. He speaks to Lotty without looking at her.)* Charlotte! It's unlike you to be late and make us have to hurry so. A wife's impunctuality always reflects poorly on the husband, I believe, if not in one way, then in another.

LOTTY. I'm sorry, Mellersh.

MELLERSH. At the least it conveys a lack of concern on her part, and, at the most, a lack of control on his.

LOTTY. Forgive me, Mellersh, but I got into a most interesting conversation at my ladies' club.

MELLERSH. That's all very well, but …

LOTTY. Do you know a gentleman from here in Hampstead by the name of Arnott?

MELLERSH. Why? What has he done?

LOTTY. Oh, nothing that I'm aware of. I'm sure he's quite the usual, in fact. I just thought you might know him through business.

MELLERSH. The name's not familiar. It will look very bad if we are late, Charlotte.

LOTTY. I am sorry, Mellersh. I wish that you would just go without me, really. You know I only feel awash with these artistic sorts.

MELLERSH. But a family solicitor must show his family, now, mustn't he? It's not so important that you enjoy yourself, but that you simply are there. *(He checks his teeth.)*

LOTTY. It's just that I always feel so … negligible. I never know what to say. And if, by chance, I do have something to say, it only comes out wrong.

MELLERSH. If you're asked for your opinion, you need merely say "marvelous," or something of that nature, and leave it at that.

That's all they want to hear anyhow. Try it.

LOTTY. "Marvelous."

MELLERSH. You'll be surprised how far it will get you.

LOTTY. It's Impressionists again, then?

MELLERSH. Why?

LOTTY. It's all just a bit of a muddle. To my eye.

MELLERSH. Sometimes one has to step back a bit. Have you tried that?

LOTTY. And then what?

MELLERSH. And then ... "Marvelous." It's not so much the artists I'm interested in, anyhow, but their patrons and sponsors, who might be in need of legal counsel.

LOTTY. I understand. Might we go to dinner after?

MELLERSH. We will eat at home. Where have you put my *Times*, Charlotte?

LOTTY. "Times," Mellersh?

MELLERSH. Yes.

LOTTY. You mean the newspaper?

MELLERSH. Of course the ... have you taken leave of your senses? What else would I mean by "my *Times*"?

LOTTY. *(Busying herself nervously.)* Of course that's what you meant. *(Mellersh waits.)*

MELLERSH. Well?

LOTTY. Well what, Mellersh?

MELLERSH. *(Steadying himself.)* Where have you put today's *Times*?

LOTTY. It seems I forgot to pick one up. *(Mellersh eyes her, Lotty moves on.)*

MELLERSH. I shall miss it now.

LOTTY. Yes. Perhaps it would be best if, in future, you picked up your own *Times*.

MELLERSH. But you pick up my *Times*, Charlotte. I see no reason to change procedure now. You need merely be sure to remember.

LOTTY. Yes, but ...

MELLERSH. *(Raising a hand.)* Case closed, my dear. Case closed. *(Lotty boils.)*

LOTTY. Mellersh?

MELLERSH. Yes?

LOTTY. Do you know what the weather is like in Italy in April?

MELLERSH. Quite lovely, I imagine. Why do you ask?

LOTTY. Oh, no reason, really. We were just talking about it today. About holidays.

MELLERSH. And what were you discussing about holidays?

LOTTY. Just that they must be nice, that's all.

MELLERSH. I'm certain they are. Although I have heard some shocking stories to the contrary. There is an inherent element of risk in holidays that colors quite nicely the sureties of home. *(Lotty thinks.)*

LOTTY. The piano needs tuning.

MELLERSH. What made you think of that?

LOTTY. I don't know. It doesn't matter. Unless you think I should tune it myself.

MELLERSH. Charlotte.

LOTTY. I'm ready, Mellersh. *(Mellersh looks up. Lotty is glowing with thrift.)*

MELLERSH. Right, then.

LOTTY. Do I look all right, Mellersh?

MELLERSH. Fine, fine. You do manage quite well with your dress allowance, my dear. Your ability with thrift is highly admirable.

LOTTY. The sureties of home.

MELLERSH. And much appreciated for it. *(He kisses two fingers and touches her nose.)*

LOTTY. Off we go, then. *(Starts to exit.)*

MELLERSH. *(Taken aback.)* Charlotte?!

LOTTY. Yes, Mellersh? *(Mellersh stares expectantly. Lotty waits, suddenly realizes.)* How silly of me. *(She goes to him, ties his tie. Mellersh thinks, quite used to being attended to.)*

MELLERSH. Do you think this Arnott is someone I should look up?

LOTTY. Oh, no. I didn't mean that. I don't know anything about him, really. I only met his wife, that's all.

MELLERSH. Well, that's very clever of you. You can make many connections for me at your ladies' club, I imagine, if you steer your conversation in a useful direction.

LOTTY. Yes, Mellersh, I'm sure. *(Mellersh thinks.)*

MELLERSH. I will miss my *Times*, Charlotte.

LOTTY. I am sorry. There shall be another tomorrow. *(Mellersh sighs with great patience. The tie is tied.)* There.

MELLERSH. Right, then. Now ... *(Takes a monocle from his pocket, places it, poses.)* How do I look? *(Lotty looks him over.)*

LOTTY. Marvelous. *(Thunder.)*

## Scene 3

*Rain. The Arnott home. A table, two chairs, a coat rack with coats and umbrellas. Frederick Arnott stands at an unseen mirror, tying his tie, preparing himself for a social engagement. He is jovial and in a party mood, singing "Ma, He's Making Eyes At Me" to himself between poses. Rose enters, returning from the club.*

ROSE. *(Surprised, disapproving.)* Frederick.

FREDERICK. Rose.

ROSE. You're here.

FREDERICK. Here I am.

ROSE. And there you go, it seems. Who is it tonight?

FREDERICK. The Bacon-Cateses. A party for my new book.

ROSE. *(Coldly.)* That should be a posh set.

FREDERICK. Hurry and you can join me.

ROSE. Wouldn't that be comical. *(Frederick picks up a book and pen.)*

FREDERICK. *Madame DuBarry* has all the appearance of being my most successful book yet, even more so than *Pompadour.* The Bacon-Cateses never invited me for *Madame Pompadour. (He opens the book and signs.)* Sin must have taken a step up in respectability if even the Bacon-Cateses have asked for the pleasure of meeting "Mr. Florian Ayers."

ROSE. Sin cannot take a step up, Frederick. And you know how I feel about that name.

FREDERICK. *(Rolling the name off of his tongue.)* "Florian Ayers." Even you must admit that as a pen name, it is most imaginative.

ROSE. Your imagination has never been in question.

FREDERICK. Yes. Well, don't dislike that name too much, darling. When God comes to browse through my literary *oeuvre,* He'll damn "Florian Ayers" straight to Hell, but you and I shall be spared. *(He smiles. Rose does not respond.)* There was a time when you laughed at my humor, Rose. You could light up a room when you laughed.

ROSE. That was before.

FREDERICK. Before my books, you mean? My poetry never afforded charity. Your church should be thanking Madame DuBarry. Those boots you bought the schoolchildren this winter? Stout with sin.

ROSE. I didn't mean your books. *(She thinks.)* You were a good poet, Frederick. And Frederick Arnott is a good name.

FREDERICK. To whom?

ROSE. To me.

FREDERICK. Rose. I am a weak and wicked man. I wish you could forgive me that.

ROSE. You are not wicked, Frederick.

FREDERICK. You're right. "Florian Ayers" is wicked. I'm merely weak.

ROSE. It's just … one should not write books God would not like to read. *(Frederick laughs.)*

FREDERICK. Madame DuBarry has nothing over Mary Magdalene, I assure you.

ROSE. Is everything funny to you?

FREDERICK. No darling, it's not. God knows.

ROSE. Does He? We are judged by our actions, Frederick, not by our intentions.

FREDERICK. He's keeping score you say?

ROSE. Something like that.

FREDERICK. And what of those who say we are loved all the more for our … humanness? *(Rose considers.)*

ROSE. I would say that they are mistaken. *(Moving toward him.)* Here. You've muffed your tie.

FREDERICK. *(Pulling away.)* I have it. *(Rose thinks.)*

ROSE. Do you know anyone by the name of Wilton?

FREDERICK. Wilton?

ROSE. A solicitor and his wife. *(Frederick shudders.)*

FREDERICK. I make quite a point of avoiding solicitors.

ROSE. I met the wife today. A most unusual woman.

FREDERICK. *(Enthused.)* Really?

ROSE. She spoke of heaven and home.

FREDERICK. *(Disappointed.)* Oh. *(He starts to sing to himself.)*

ROSE. And of loss. She claims to see things. She said that I looked to her like a disappointed Madonna. *(Frederick pauses momentarily, thinking, resumes singing.)* What is that exactly?

FREDERICK. What is what?

ROSE. The song you're singing.

FREDERICK. Just a little jazz number I've heard. *(Sings to Rose, dancing.)* "Ma, he's making eyes at me! Ma, he's awful nice to me!"

ROSE. "Making eyes"?

FREDERICK. Yes. You know ... *(He shoots her a seductive stare.)* Valentino. *(Rose finds the image a bit more appealing than she'd like.)* ROSE. Chaplin, perhaps. *(She turns away, thinks.)* This Mrs. Wilton. She wondered how one is to go forward when so much has been lost. FREDERICK. *(Concerned.)* Exactly what did the two of you discuss? ROSE. Nothing specific. I'm not at all certain she heard a word I said, actually. FREDERICK. *(Sincerely.)* Rose. My book tour lasts from the end of March through all of April. Come with me. ROSE. *(Looking at him, moved.)* April? With you? *(Considers.)* As what? "Mrs Florian Ayers"? Really, you and Mrs. Wilton are two of a kind. *(She hands him the book.)* You don't want to miss your party. FREDERICK. No. *(He gets his hat, starts to exit, defeated.)* Rose? Should the things you have faith in ever include the people who love you ... *(He pops his hat on his head.)* ... be in touch. *(Thunder.)*

## Scene 4

*Rain. A church. Rose is searching for something. Lotty enters, glancing over her shoulder.*

LOTTY. *(Whispering loudly.)* Mrs. Arnott! Rose!
ROSE. *(Aghast.)* Mrs. Wilton!
LOTTY. I've only a moment. I told Mellersh I left my gloves in our pew.
ROSE. Lying to your husband, Mrs. Wilton, in Our Father's house?
LOTTY. Oh, but I didn't lie. I really left them, so that I wouldn't be lying. *(She retrieves her gloves. Rose looks heavenward.)* I got it, Rose! A reply to our inquiry about the castle!
ROSE. *(Sternly.)* Please. We really must talk.
LOTTY. It is most kind, from a Mr. Antony Wilding, of Knightsbridge. It smells of cinnamon!
ROSE. Cinnamon?
LOTTY. Isn't that delightful! But, brace yourself. Sixty pounds for the month of April.
ROSE. Mrs. Wilton ...

LOTTY. I know it would be a stretch for us both.

ROSE. Corresponding with someone we know nothing of. We've gone too far already.

LOTTY. Rose.

ROSE. And all of this talk of money. Please. It has, indeed, been grand dreaming of this. But no further.

LOTTY. But, Rose.

ROSE. *(Taking a stand.)* I have made up my mind, Mrs. Wilton.

LOTTY. Lotty. If it's only the money, then I have an idea.

ROSE. It is not only the money.

LOTTY. I thought perhaps if we advertise for traveling companions …

ROSE. Companions?

LOTTY. Ladies. There must be dozens of ladies in our situation who would enjoy sharing such a holiday. Not that we'd want dozens, of course. But another couple, say, would certainly ease the burden.

ROSE. Please … we really mustn't discuss this here. It's wrong. I feel as if we're plotting.

LOTTY. But we are! Plotting our escape! Have you lost something?

ROSE. One of the schoolchildren somehow misplaced his boots and stockings during services. *(Lotty laughs.)*

LOTTY. "Put thy shoes from off thy feet, for this is holy ground."

ROSE. Angus O'Shea is no Moses. As any number of schoolgirls will tell you.

LOTTY. Rose …

ROSE. You've taken leave of your senses, Mrs. Wilton.

LOTTY. Don't say that!

ROSE. Start with your nest egg. What if there is an actual need?

LOTTY. This is an actual need.

ROSE. I don't want to hear any more.

LOTTY. But Rose … if we don't go forward … well … *(Inspired.)* …we will be depriving two perfectly innocent traveling companions of their holiday. Two good, unhappy ladies like ourselves. Perhaps in even greater need than ourselves. *(Rose considers.)*

ROSE. *(Strongly.)* You are a bully, Mrs. Wilton!

LOTTY. Meet me at the club on Wednesday for tea.

ROSE. Yes. No!

LOTTY. We can compose our advert.

ROSE. Mrs. Wilton!

LOTTY. Lotty, Rose. You really must call me Lotty.

ROSE. We are not placing an advertisement, because we are not responding to Mr. Wilding.

LOTTY. But I have.

ROSE. What?

LOTTY. I have sent him my nest egg, as a deposit.

ROSE. *(Stunned.)* Lotty.

LOTTY. It is done, Rose. The castle is ours! *(Thunder. They look heavenward.)* Have you told your husband?

ROSE. Of course not.

LOTTY. We should tell them. Even Moses asked permission.

ROSE. *(Near tears.)* Please stop talking about Moses.

LOTTY. You're right. It's more like David and Goliath. Rose. All I'm asking for is your faith. *(Mellersh calls from outside.)*

MELLERSH. *(Offstage.)* Charlotte!

LOTTY. Gad! It's Goliath. Wednesday! *(She starts to exit.)*

ROSE. *(Lost.)* Husbands, Lotty! *(Lotty stops.)*

LOTTY. What?

ROSE. Husbands.

LOTTY. Yes. Isn't it terrible. But who could resist an invitation to heaven? *(Imagining.)* "Two ladies seek other ladies who appreciate ... " *(Blend to Scene 5.)*

## Scene 5

*The home of Caroline Bramble. A table, three chairs, a coat rack with coats and umbrellas. Caroline enters, reading from the* Times.

CAROLINE. " ... seek other ladies who appreciate wisteria and sunshine." *(Lotty and Rose sit attentively. Caroline wears a loose, colorful silk négligée. Her youthfulness shines through a weary air. She prepares a glass of aspirin powder and lights a cigarette, clearly hung over.)*

LOTTY. We were so pleased to receive your reply, Lady Bramble. Although we never expected that our advertisement would attract someone ... such as yourself.

CAROLINE. Oh?

ROSE. We've read about you often in the newspapers, Lady

17

Bramble. Your life seems so ... full.

CAROLINE. *(With chilly aloofness.)* Yes.

ROSE. You do realize that the castle is very quiet and remote.

CAROLINE. I hope so. Is there a telephone?

LOTTY. No.

CAROLINE. Good.

ROSE. Mrs. Wilton was telling me, in fact, Lady Bramble, of something she read about your dancing on tables.

CAROLINE. In Paris.

ROSE. Really.

LOTTY. You must be very tired. *(Explaining herself.)* Whenever I see moderns such as yourself I always see a certain ... weariness. Modernity being such a shifty beast.

CAROLINE. *(Uncertain.)* Yes. Have you received many replies to your advertisement?

ROSE. To our surprise, I'm afraid, only two.

LOTTY. The other is from a Mrs. Clayton Graves. Do you know her, Lady Bramble?

CAROLINE. I don't believe so.

LOTTY. You know so many people.

CAROLINE. That's just it, I'm afraid. Mother insists on my knowing everyone, or at least on everyone she knows knowing me. She fancies herself a "patroness of the arts," which for her simply means the chance to give parties. An opportunistic group, artists. They never miss a party. Always grabbing and making eyes. Now she's collecting writers, the sorriest lot yet. Trying to create what's lacking in their own lives. Do you know any writers?

LOTTY. No. *(They look to Rose, who looks away.)*

CAROLINE. I'm in great need of an escape right now. From all of it.

LOTTY. We are of like minds, then, Lady Bramble. Mrs. Arnott and myself are escaping too!

ROSE. Lotty.

CAROLINE. Escaping? *(Joking.)* You aren't "wanted women," are you?

LOTTY. *(Laughing.)* Oh, Lady Bramble! We're not wanted at all! We're just in need of a holiday, that's all. And I believe the castle will be the perfect place.

CAROLINE. Yes. It seemed so to me as well. I had replied to the original advertisement, actually, but was answered that someone had already placed a deposit.

LOTTY. I do hope we haven't spoiled your plans, Lady Bramble.

CAROLINE. Oh, I really didn't care. A month alone had seemed appealing. But strange surroundings and simple company may prove most acceptable.
ROSE. *(Smoothly.)* We may pale in comparison with your usual acquaintances, Lady Bramble, but I assure you that Mrs. Wilton and myself are by no means "simple."
CAROLINE. *(Unusually uncertain.)* Oh, I never meant that you were. What I meant was ...
LOTTY. No grabbing!
CAROLINE. *(Relieved.)* Precisely. What I really meant, I suppose, is that you aren't ... men.
LOTTY. *(Smiling.)* Yes.
ROSE. *(Not smiling.)* That is true.
CAROLINE. With men it would be impossible to be as ... unrestricted as I'd like. *(She stretches, revealing a silky chemise.)*
ROSE. Unrestricted?
CAROLINE. Part of what intrigued me about your advertisement is that it would be quite a novelty, really, to be among lady friends. I haven't many.
LOTTY. Oh?
ROSE. And why do you think that is, Lady Bramble?
CAROLINE. Perhaps at the end of April you could tell me. Should I join you. *(Thunder.)* Isn't this rain a nuisance?
LOTTY. *(Feeling a kinship.)* Oh, yes!
CAROLINE. May I offer you a cognac?
ROSE. It is eleven in the morning, Lady Bramble.
CAROLINE. Yes. *(With a hint of sadness.)* May I ask you something?
LOTTY. Of course, Lady Bramble.
CAROLINE. Were your husbands lost?
ROSE. Lost?
CAROLINE. In the war.
LOTTY. Well, no, Lady Bramble.
ROSE. Our husbands have not been lost at all, Lady Bramble.
CAROLINE. *(Relieved.)* Oh! Isn't that funny? You look like widows! Had I seen you on a street corner, I would have been inclined to give you a donation.
ROSE. *(Beginning to boil.)* Lady Bramble ...
CAROLINE. I should like to join you at the castle, then.
LOTTY. Grand! *(Rose scowls.)*
CAROLINE. *(Aware of Rose.)* And, should we find that things

19

don't work out, I shall simply move on and you may keep my payment in full.

ROSE. But that would be unfair to you, Lady Bramble.

LOTTY. But things will work out, Lady Bramble. You'll see. I'm quite sure we're all going to be the very best of friends. Better than friends! Sisters!

CAROLINE. *(Warily.)* Yes. Well, let's start then by not calling me Lady Bramble. Mother is Lady Bramble. Call me Lady Caroline.

LOTTY. *(Beaming.)* Lady Caroline!

CAROLINE. Well. *(She lifts her hand in a graceful salute.)* All'Italia! *(Lotty and Rose stare, perplexed. Caroline explains.)* To Italy. *(Lotty smiles and lifts her hand, fumbling enthusiastically.)*

LOTTY. All'Italia! *(They look at Rose. She frowns, considers, lifts a fist with stiff reluctance. Thunder.)*


# Scene 6


*Rain. The home of Mrs. Graves. A table, three chairs, a coat rack with coats and umbrellas. Lotty and Rose are seated, silent. Mrs. Graves paces imperiously. She is heavily dressed, highly proper, and walks with the aid of a stick.*


MRS. GRAVES. If we are to spend the whole of a month together, I consider it preferable that certain ground rules be spelled out sooner rather than later. I do not approve of modern language, behavior or thinking. I find informal idioms of speech unacceptable, and will not tolerate them. I take breakfast promptly at seven in the morning, luncheon at noon, tea at half past four, and dinner at quarter to eight. I like nuts. I am not interested in idle conversation. My only desire is to sit quietly and remember.

ROSE. Yes, well ...

MRS. GRAVES. *(Not listening, sitting down to a bowl of nuts.)* Although I have great fondness for the Italian seaside, I have no fondness whatsoever for those native customs so many find charming. I would expect such behavior to remain outside of our retreat.

LOTTY. Yes, I'm sure ...

MRS. GRAVES. Now to which of you does the castle belong?

LOTTY. Oh, to none of us, Mrs. Graves. We haven't even seen it. It was advertised. Mrs. Arnott and I have rented it.

MRS. GRAVES. *(Appalled.)* Rented?! How do you know it isn't a dilapidation?

ROSE. We've corresponded with the owner, a Mr. Antony Wilding. It appears to be most agreeable.

LOTTY. There's a private beach, and olive groves, and bushels and bushels of wisteria. *(Mrs. Graves thinks, cracks open a nut.)*

MRS. GRAVES. I am very fond of wisteria. The house at Box Hill was covered with it. I remember once my father and I ...

LOTTY. Your father lived at Box Hill, Mrs. Graves?

MRS. GRAVES. Of course not. George Meredith lived at Box Hill. The writer. My father often took me there on invitation.

ROSE. You knew George Meredith, Mrs. Graves?

MRS. GRAVES. My father traveled among all the great men. *(She rises, points her stick at unseen portraits.)* Carlyle. Arnold. Tennyson.

LOTTY. Tennyson, Rose. Imagine!

MRS. GRAVES. As I was saying ...

LOTTY. *(Pointing.)* Is that a photograph of Tennyson, Mrs. Graves?

MRS. GRAVES. No. That is a photograph of Mr. Clayton Graves, my late husband. A sizable difference, I assure you. *(Raises her stick. Lotty and Rose flinch.) That* is Tennyson. And I am the young girl with the pigtail. Which, I might add, gave the great one no small delight. He would often tell my father ...

LOTTY. *(Excitedly.)* Did you know Keats, Mrs. Graves?

ROSE. Lotty! *(Mrs. Graves freezes.)*

MRS. GRAVES. Keats?!

LOTTY. Yes. John Keats. The poet.

MRS. GRAVES. I am well aware ... *(Frigidly.)* I did not know Keats, Mrs. Wilton.

LOTTY. Oh.

MRS. GRAVES. And if that is the direction in which you are heading, I regret to inform you that I was also unacquainted with Shakespeare.

LOTTY. Of course. The immortals seem so alive, don't they? One forgets sometimes that they are dead.

MRS. GRAVES. Many for quite some time.

LOTTY. It was just that I thought I saw Keats the other day.

ROSE. Lotty!

MRS. GRAVES. Saw Keats?!

LOTTY. Yes. Crossing the street in Hampstead, in front of his house.

ROSE. Mrs. Graves …

LOTTY. But then I suppose it was his ghost, naturally. *(Mrs. Graves eyes Lotty, who looks at Rose, who looks away, pained.)*

MRS. GRAVES. Do you have references?

ROSE. Shouldn't we be the ones asking for references from you, Mrs. Graves?

MRS. GRAVES. *(Surprised that this has come from Rose. Gathering all of her dignity.)* If you must, you may communicate with the President of the Royal Academy, the Archbishop of Canterbury, and the Governor of the Bank of England.

ROSE. I see.

LOTTY. *(Rising, deflecting.)* Is the large portrait of your father, Mrs. Graves?

MRS. GRAVES. Yes. That is himself. But we were speaking of references, Mrs. Wilton.

LOTTY. And the other portrait is your mother?

MRS. GRAVES. My mother?! That, Mrs. Wilton, is the good Queen Victoria.

LOTTY. I don't think references are nice things between decent English women. We needn't distrust each other. We're not Americans.

ROSE. *(Rising.)* References bring an atmosphere into our holiday plan that isn't quite what we want, Mrs. Graves. Good day. *(She pushes Lotty toward the exit.)*

MRS. GRAVES. How are the expenses to be divided?

LOTTY. *(Excitedly.)* Fifteen pounds each for rent, plus food. A real bargain!

MRS. GRAVES. I'm an old woman. I don't eat much.

ROSE. That would certainly be your choice to make, Mrs. Graves.

LOTTY. Perhaps we can catch our own, Mrs. Graves. How are you with a bow? *(Mrs. Graves is stricken again.)*

MRS. GRAVES. Your advertisement clearly stated that there would be a cook. My stick prohibits me from entering kitchens.

ROSE. There is a woman by the name of Costanza. *(Ko-stahn-zah.)*

MRS. GRAVES. Costan…? Fifteen pounds. Really, ten seems most reasonable, considering the circumstances.

ROSE. Fifteen, Mrs. Graves.

LOTTY. Fifteen is fair, Mrs. Graves.

MRS. GRAVES. The wisteria is guaranteed?

ROSE. Look …

LOTTY. Mrs. Graves, Mr. Wilding has assured us that we shall have wisteria.

MRS. GRAVES. *(With great reluctance.)* I shall waive references. But no wisteria and I'll expect a deduction. *(Sits.)*

ROSE. Thank you, Mrs. Graves. You've been most ... *(Mrs. Graves gestures for them to sit. They obey.)* I can't seem to find the word I'm looking for.

MRS. GRAVES. Is the fourth of our party a widow as well? *(Lotty and Rose look at each other, perplexed.)*

LOTTY. A widow, Mrs. Graves? Well, no. Actually ... *(Mrs. Graves raises her hand for silence.)*

MRS. GRAVES. *(Gravely.)* All in good time. All in good time. *(Reciting, frighteningly.)* "Old sisters of a day gone by / Gray nurses, loving nothing new / Why should they miss their yearly due / Before their time? They too will die." *(Lotty and Rose cower. Mrs. Graves cracks a nut, smiles.)* May I offer you a nut? *(Thunder.)*

## Scene 7

*Rain. The flat of Antony Wilding. A table, two chairs, a coat rack with coats and umbrellas. Lotty and Rose stand attentively.*

WILDING. Oh yes, the wisteria is everywhere, as advertised. You can see some of the view in these photographs here. *(The ladies turn their eyes away from Wilding himself, who wears a loose, open shirt and an even more open smile.)* I took these myself, I'm afraid. You'd hardly mistake them for professionals. *(He turns the photo. They huddle together, turning their heads.)* It's a small castle, but of course it has most of the "modern improvements," as an estate agent would say. Its name is *San Salvatore. (Salvator-ay.)*

LOTTY and ROSE. *(Trying it out.)* San Salvatore.

LOTTY. It sounds sacred, Rose.

ROSE. What is that there, Mr. Wilding?

WILDING. *(Looking at Rose, distracted by something in her face.)* What, Mrs. Arnott?

ROSE. *(Pointing.)* That. *(He continues to stare, pulls himself away to look at the photo.)*

WILDING. That, I'm afraid, appears to have been my left thumb.

*(The ladies smile discreetly.)* But had it not been there, it would be a view of the sea and of the lower garden. The castle has both upper and lower gardens, with a lovely terrace between. *(He hands them a card.)* For you. A postcard of the village below.

LOTTY and ROSE. *(Reading.)* Mez-zago.

WILDING. *(To Rose, enunciating.)* Met-zago.

ROSE. *(Self-consciously.)* Met-zago. *(Wilding smiles.)*

WILDING. I like your face, Mrs. Arnott. *(Rose freezes.)* But here, let's make you comfortable. *(He removes their coats.)* In April, you know, the area is simply a mass of flowers. *(Admiring Rose's figure. To her.)* You must wear white.

ROSE. *(Embarrassed.)* White?

WILDING. Yes. There's a dock and small boat, if … well, if your husbands are so inclined.

LOTTY. Our husbands, Mr. Wilding? *(In mock mourning.)* Our husbands, I'm afraid … will not be with us.

WILDING. Forgive me. So many widows these days.

ROSE. No …

LOTTY. There will be four of us, however. Lady friends.

WILDING. Really? *San Salvatore* should be filled with friends. It can be a bit lonely.

ROSE. Is *San Salvatore* a family home?

WILDING. Yes. Or it was. I've no longer any family, so it's no longer a home, I suppose.

LOTTY. Oh.

WILDING. Father's parents had the place built. A love nest of sorts, from the way he told it. I never knew them, unfortunately, but some of the stories are delightful.

LOTTY. It sounds wonderful.

WILDING. *(At Rose.)* Yes. It's beautiful. *(Pulling away.)* Father loved the place. Mother never cared for it much, really, until her later years alone. And then, while I was away in the Army, she and *San Salvatore* seemed to become one.

LOTTY. Where did you serve, Mr. Wilding? *(His smile fades.)*

WILDING. Flanders, mostly.

LOTTY. *(Sincerely.)* Brave battles.

ROSE. We are indebted to you, Mr. Wilding. *(Wilding nods.)*

WILDING. I lost Mother last year, sad to say. She always said that there was something enchanted about the castle in April. I hate to miss it this year, but I've work in Rome.

ROSE. What is your work, Mr. Wilding?

WILDING. I paint. Portraits. Classical, of course. Two eyes, one mouth, and so on. *(Lotty thinks.)*

LOTTY. Marvelous!

WILDING. I've a studio in Bloomsbury. Perhaps you both could visit sometime and be studied. I'm said to have a particular talent with the female form. *(Rose lets out a small gasp. Lotty hurriedly hands an envelope to Wilding.)*

LOTTY. Our final payment, Mr. Wilding.

WILDING. Well. *(Takes the envelope.)* Now I'm richer ... *(He hugs Lotty, to her delight.)* ... and you're happier. *(He starts toward Rose, but she cringes.)* What would you say to celebrating our union, as it were, over a cup of hot tea? *(He motions for them to sit.)*

LOTTY. Oh, that would be lovely. *(Sits.)*

ROSE. That's very kind, Mr. Wilding. *(Sits.)*

WILDING. Good. Now, I have plain English black, or, for the more daring, a Moroccan blend I'm fond of with just a dash of cinnamon that goes by the rather audacious name of "Indiscreet."

LOTTY. *(Bursting out in giggles.)* Oh, my! The "Indiscreet" sounds most intriguing.

WILDING. Wonderful! And for you, Mrs. Arnott? *(Rose considers.)*

ROSE. I shall have the black.

WILDING. Right. *(Serving.)* Now you must tell me all about the friends you are taking.

ROSE. We hardly know a thing about them, really.

LOTTY. We took your lead, Mr. Wilding, and placed an advertisement.

WILDING. Oh?

LOTTY. There's Lady Caroline Bramble, who likes cognac and dancing. And Mrs. Clayton Graves, who knew Tennyson and likes ... *(Thinks.)*

ROSE. Nuts.

WILDING. How interesting. Well, I'm certain that you will all find *San Salvatore* to your liking. Mrs. Arnott, this will sound a bit extraordinary, but there is a portrait of you there.

ROSE. A portrait of me?

WILDING. Yes. A Madonna. There's one on the stairs really exactly like you. *(Rose is stunned.)*

ROSE. Well ... *(Thunder.)*

WILDING. *San Salvatore* will certainly be a nice change from this weather.

LOTTY. Yes.

WILDING. You'll find the place has lots of sunshine, whatever else it hasn't got.
ROSE. What else hasn't it got, Mr. Wilding?
WILDING. Troubles. Worries. The plumbing is a bit antique, but Costanza can help you with that. And to think you'll be among it all in only two days.
LOTTY. We leave tomorrow!
WILDING. You've squared away all of your affairs? *(Lotty and Rose share a guilty glance.)*
ROSE. A couple of things remain. *(Thunder.)*


## Scene 8


*Rain. Both the Arnott and Wilton homes. Two tables, four chairs. Rose sits alone. Mellersh sits, finishing a dessert, a napkin hanging from his collar. Lotty tends to him. The scene is of escalating fury.*


MELLERSH. Well, now. I am the fat cat tonight, aren't I? All my favorites for dinner.
LOTTY. Was everything to your liking, Mellersh?
MELLERSH. All quite delicious, my dear. One would think this was a special evening of some sort. And perhaps it is! *(Frederick enters, foggy from an evening party.)*
FREDERICK. Well, now. You're up late!
ROSE. Yes, Frederick. There's something I need to speak to you about.
LOTTY. May I speak to you about something, Mellersh?
MELLERSH. It so happens I have something to speak to you about as well. You tell me yours, and then I'll tell you mine.
FREDERICK. Could it wait until morning? Once again Mr. Ayers was a success, and once again Mr. Arnott is exhausted.
LOTTY. No. You first, Mellersh.
MELLERSH. Very well.
FREDERICK. Sometimes I think a little less attention would still do the trick, really.
ROSE. And perhaps a little less champagne.

FREDERICK. No. That helps.

MELLERSH. Do you remember last month your asking me about holidays?

LOTTY. Well, yes, Mellersh. It's funny you should mention that.

ROSE. I wonder if I might have some money.

MELLERSH. I believe it will please you to know ... that I am taking you!

FREDERICK. So that's it.

ROSE. Extra money, I mean.

LOTTY. "Taking me," Mellersh?

MELLERSH. To Italy!

FREDERICK. *(Taking out his billfold.)* What is it this time? Boots or Bibles?

ROSE. I'm going away, Frederick.

MELLERSH. Did you hear me? I said that I am taking you on holiday!

LOTTY. That is really the most extraordinary coincidence.

FREDERICK. Going away?

MELLERSH. Coincidence?

ROSE. For a rest.

LOTTY. Yes, really most extraordinary. Because I was just about to tell you that I am ... going.

ROSE. Someplace by the sea.

MELLERSH. Going? Going where?

LOTTY. To Italy.

FREDERICK. Come with me on my book tour.

MELLERSH. Have you taken leave of your senses, Charlotte?

ROSE. That is impossible, Frederick.

MELLERSH. How could you be going to Italy? Ridiculous!

FREDERICK. It is not impossible!

LOTTY. It is not ridiculous!

FREDERICK. Listen to me, Rose.

LOTTY. Listen to me, Mellersh. I've been invited.

ROSE. I've listened enough.

LOTTY. A friend has invited me. With a home there.

ROSE. I've waited enough.

LOTTY. And I am going.

FREDERICK. So have I.

MELLERSH. You have no friends ... with homes in Italy!

ROSE. So we agree then.

LOTTY. I have, Mellersh. I've mentioned her to you.

27

MELLERSH. Who?

FREDERICK. Rose?

LOTTY. Rose.

MELLERSH. Rose? *(Lotty and Rose look at each other.)*

ROSE. We can't go back, Frederick.

MELLERSH. Rose who?

ROSE. We can only go forward.

MELLERSH. You've kept secrets, Charlotte!

FREDERICK. But not alone!

MELLERSH. Secrets are like rust!

FREDERICK. It's been four years now, Rose!

MELLERSH. And now I am to believe that you are actually asking me ...

LOTTY. I am not asking you anything, Mellersh. I'm telling you!

ROSE. I *am* alone, Frederick.

FREDERICK. As am I.

MELLERSH. This is ridiculous!

FREDERICK. *(Holding out cash.)* Take your money then, Mrs. Arnott.

LOTTY. This time tomorrow I shall be on a train.

FREDERICK. I shall write up my itinerary ...

MELLERSH. Tomorrow?

LOTTY. To Italy!

FREDERICK. ... should you wish to be in contact. *(Thunder.)*

LOTTY. Damn this rain!

MELLERSH. Rain?!

FREDERICK. Just know that you were the one who closed the door, Rose.

MELLERSH. If you think you are taking one step out of that door, Mrs. Wilton.

ROSE. *(Hopelessly.)* I'm sorry, Frederick. *(She takes the money, exits.)*

LOTTY. *(Sharply.)* I'm sorry, Mellersh. *(She snatches the napkin from Mellersh's collar, exits. A train whistles loud and long. Mellersh and Frederick look at each other, stunned.)*

ANNOUNCEMENT. *Signore e signori, avere prego tutti i documenti pronti per il controllo. Grazie, e benvenuti in Italia!* ("Ladies and gentlemen, please have your papers ready for inspection. Thank you, and welcome to Italy!")

## Scene 9

*The sound of a train in motion. A train compartment. Rose reads from an Italian phrase book. Lotty sleeps. Travel bags are at their feet, coats and hats at their sides.*

ROSE. *(Gravely trying out words from the book.)* Smarrito. Mi scusi, mi sono smarrito. No. Mi sono smarri-ta. I am lost, feminine. *Mi scusi, mi sono smarrita. ("Excuse me, I am lost." Lights flash and the train whistles loudly as it passes through a tunnel. Lotty awakens, frightened.)*
LOTTY. Mellersh!
ROSE. *(Nervously.)* It was only a tunnel, Lotty. Tunnel. *(She thumbs through the book.)* Tunnel.
LOTTY. *(Looking out of the compartment window.)* Have we crossed the Italian border?
ROSE. I can't tell. It's so dark out. We're running so late.
LOTTY. I wish we were there.
ROSE. We are in God's hands now, Lotty.
LOTTY. I can't see a thing. Why is the window damp?
ROSE. It's raining. *(Lotty nearly loses all hope.)*
LOTTY. I'm sure Italian rain is better than English rain.
ROSE. We were expected hours ago. We'll never find our way alone.
LOTTY. When we get to Genoa, Mr. Wilding said we need merely ask for *Mez-zago.*
ROSE. *Met-zago.*
LOTTY. Why do they pronounce it *"Met-zago"*? It doesn't have a "t." *(She takes the book from Rose, looks through it.)*
ROSE. *(Adrift.)* You're certain you saw us at *San Salvatore*, Lotty?
LOTTY. Yes, Rose.
ROSE. And Lady Caroline and Mrs. Graves? Did you also see them?
LOTTY. No. I didn't.
ROSE. They aren't the ladies I would have chosen.
LOTTY. Perhaps they've been chosen for us. When we get to *San Salvatore*, let's prepare everything for them, shall we? Make things perfect for their arrival.
ROSE. That would be proper.
LOTTY. We can choose the rooms that would please them, and

29

fill them with flowers.

ROSE. If there *are* flowers.

LOTTY. There will be. There must be. *(They look out, lost. Train sounds steadily increase.)*

ROSE. What is the Italian for "help"?

LOTTY. Oh, Rose.

ROSE. Please, Lotty. Look it up. *(Lotty does so. Rose stands, panicking.)* How do we stop the train?

LOTTY. We can't stop the train, Rose.

ROSE. *(Dressing.)* I'm sure if we simply explain that there has been a dreadful mistake.

LOTTY. This is not a mistake!

ROSE. *(Forcefully irate.)* I told you that I was a happy individual. And I was. I am. Happy! But you spoke of peace. And ... and of sisters. And ... and cinnamon! And you got my head quite turned around. You're not a hummingbird at all, Lotty Wilton. You're a hawk! Clear-eyed and ... and ... Why aren't you dressing?! *(Lotty holds up the book.)*

LOTTY. *"Aiuto."*

ROSE. What?

LOTTY. The Italian for "help." *"Aiuto."* *(Rose crumbles, sitting.)*

ROSE. *(Adrift.)* Aiuto. *(The ladies fall silent, lost in thought.)*

LOTTY. It isn't fair, Rose. To think that we ought to be so happy now, and we're not. *(Sighs.)* Husbands.

ROSE. *(Sighs.)* Husbands. *(Train sounds rise. Rose begins to pray.)* Aiuto. Mi sono smarrita.

LOTTY. It's going to be lovely, Rose.

ROSE. *Mi scusi!*

LOTTY. It's going to be heaven.

ROSE. *(Dropping to her knees.)* Perdonna me!

LOTTY. Sunshine!

ROSE. *Aiuto!*

LOTTY. Wisteria!

ROSE. *Aiuto! (Another tunnel. Lotty drops to her knees in fright, begins praying.)*

LOTTY. *Aiuto!*

ROSE. What have we done, Lotty? What have we done?!

LOTTY. I don't know, Rose. But whatever it is ... *(Lotty and Rose look at each other, lost.)* ... we've done it! *(The train whistle screams as darkness envelops them.)*

## End of Act One

# ACT TWO

## Scene 1

*Lights up on the terrace at San Salvatore, the following morning. A table and chairs, a chaise. Exits from the terrace into the villa and into the garden. The impression of beautiful garden surroundings, sunshine. Costanza sits at the table, singing to herself, snapping beans and placing them in a large bowl. She is dressed in simple, comfortable clothing and sandals. Caroline reclines on the chaise in a thin summer ensemble, reading a book. Mrs. Graves enters from the villa, carrying a small pitcher. She walks with her stick and is dressed much too warmly for the weather, from high-buttoned shoes to a rather imposing hat. She holds out the pitcher.*

MRS. GRAVES. What is this?! *(Caroline and Costanza shiver, their patience already waning.)*
COSTANZA. *(Looking heavenward.)* Santa Maria! *(Sighs, resigned.) Cosa ho fatto adesso, Signora? Qual'è il problema adesso?* ("What have I done now, Madame? What problem have you found now?")
MRS. GRAVES. You may rattle on and on all you wish, my friend, and I still will not understand you. I speak only the Italian of Dante.
COSTANZA. *Cosa c'è? Qual'è l'argomento?* ("What is it? What is the matter?")
MRS. GRAVES. Lady Caroline, would you please determine from Costanza the origin of this milk. *(Costanza gets up to look at the contents of the pitcher.)*
CAROLINE. The "origin," Mrs. Graves?
MRS. GRAVES. Yes. *(Costanza takes the pitcher.)*
CAROLINE. You mean the vendor?
MRS. GRAVES. I mean the animal. *(Mrs. Graves goes to the table, pulls playing cards and a large bell from her pockets, staking her claim.)*
COSTANZA. *(To Caroline.) Il latte è buono, Donna Carolina.* ("The milk is good.")

CAROLINE. *Sì, sì. La Signora vorrebbe sapere che tipo di latte è questo, Costanza. ("The lady would like to know what kind of milk this is.")*

COSTANZA. *Che tipo di latte, Signorina? Non capisco. È latte! ("What kind of milk, Miss? I don't understand. It's milk!")*

CAROLINE. *La signora vorrebbe sapere ... l'animale. ("The lady would like to know the animal.")*

COSTANZA. *L'animale? ("The animal?" She eyes Mrs. Graves.)* Eh! *Una mucca, naturalmente, Donna Carolina. ("A cow, of course.")*

CAROLINE. *Sì, grazie, Costanza. Sono spiacente per il problema. ("I'm sorry for the problem.")*

COSTANZA. *(Already charmed by Caroline.) Il problema non è con voi, Signorina. ("The problem is not with you, Miss." She eyes Mrs. Graves. Under her breath.) Animale! (She retrieves the bowl and exits into the villa.)*

MRS. GRAVES. *(Sitting.)* What was she saying?

CAROLINE. Nothing of concern. Cow.

MRS. GRAVES. What?!

CAROLINE. It is cow's milk. It seems Italian milk also comes from cows. *(She rises to retrieve another pillow, returns to the chaise.)*

MRS. GRAVES. You look as if you had nothing on underneath.

CAROLINE. I haven't.

MRS. GRAVES. How very imprudent. And how highly improper.

CAROLINE. But there are no men here, so how can it be improper? Have you noticed how difficult it is to be improper without men?

MRS. GRAVES. God, Lady Caroline, we have been assured, is a man. *(Lotty rushes from the villa in a white nightgown, barefooted and wide-eyed. She looks out at the gardens and sea, but then sees Caroline and Mrs. Graves.)*

LOTTY. Oh!

CAROLINE. Good morning.

LOTTY. Lady Caroline!

MRS. GRAVES. *(Disapprovingly.)* You've arrived.

LOTTY. Mrs. Graves. Yes, late last night. But ...

MRS. GRAVES. Without clothing, apparently. *(Rose rushes in, also in a white nightgown, also barefooted and wide-eyed, clutching her Italian phrase book. She sees Caroline and Mrs. Graves and is embarrassed.)*

ROSE. Oh! Ladies! Excuse me!

LOTTY. Yes, excuse us, Mrs. Graves, Lady Caroline. We hadn't thought you'd arrived.

CAROLINE. Here we are!

LOTTY. Yes. Not that we're not happy to see you. It's just a great disappointment. *(Caroline and Mrs. Graves glance at each other, questioning.)*

ROSE. What Lotty means is that we'd planned to give you such a welcome. We were going to choose the nicest rooms for you.

CAROLINE. We've done that.

ROSE. And we meant to make them pretty for you with flowers.

MRS. GRAVES. Costanza has seen to everything. In her way.

CAROLINE. Mrs. Graves and I arrived yesterday morning. *(Wincing.)* Together.

LOTTY. *(Looking out, entranced.)* Look at this place, Rose. When I woke this morning, I prepared myself to accept whatever I found. But I couldn't have imagined. The flowers! Snapdragons and periwinkles! Daphnes and iris! And lavender! And cherry trees! And wisteria, Mrs. Graves, simply tumbling over itself!

MRS. GRAVES. *(Disappointed.)* Yes.

LOTTY. And sunshine! *(She raises her face to the sun.)* Heaven! Look up "heaven," Rose. *(Rose opens the phrase book, does so. A distant church bell rings. Lotty drinks it in.)* Listen! Their church bell sounds so light and inviting! Our church bell never sounded like that. *(Mrs. Graves rings her bell furiously. The ladies jump.)*

MRS. GRAVES. *(Bellowing.)* Costanza!

ROSE. It appears you two have everything under control.

MRS. GRAVES. It does save time.

LOTTY. Rose! Remember Mr. Wilding said that there was an upstairs sitting room with a view. Let's go first thing after breakfast. I suddenly want to write to everyone I know!

MRS. GRAVES. That is *my* sitting room, Mrs. Wilton.

LOTTY. *Your* sitting room?

MRS. GRAVES. I am an old woman. I need a place to myself.

ROSE. But it is a sitting room, Mrs. Graves.

MRS. GRAVES. There is another room you and Mrs. Wilton may use downstairs at the back next to Costanza's room. I must have quiet. *(She rings the bell.)* Your bedrooms were acceptable?

LOTTY. Oh …

ROSE. Cozy.

MRS. GRAVES. There were two beds in my room, filling it up unnecessarily, so I had one taken out. It has made it much more agreeable.

LOTTY. That's why I have two beds in my room.

ROSE.  I have two in mine as well.

MRS. GRAVES.  Yours must be Lady Caroline's second bed. She also had hers removed.

LOTTY.  I see. What was it, Rose?

ROSE.  What?

LOTTY.  *(Weakly.)* "Heaven." *(Rose returns to the book.)* You are chic, Lady Caroline.

MRS. GRAVES.  She needs a hat. One mustn't get too much sun too soon, Mrs. Wilton.

ROSE.  *(Finding the word. Flatly.)* "Paradiso." Heaven. *(Costanza enters from the villa.)*

COSTANZA.  *(Seeing Lotty and Rose, pleased.)* Ah, buona mattina, Signore! Scusatemi. *("Good morning, ladies! Excuse me." Stone-faced to Mrs. Graves.)* Sì, Signora? *("Yes, Madame?")*

MRS. GRAVES.  It is time for breakfast.

COSTANZA.  *Adesso? ("Now?")*

MRS. GRAVES.  *(Shouting.)* Breakfast!

COSTANZA.  *Sì, sì, Signora.* "Breakfast." *(Instructing.)* "Colazione." *(Mrs. Graves waves her away.) Imperialista! (She exits.)*

MRS. GRAVES.  I saw to it breakfast was delayed one hour for your first day. It will not be done again. *(Standing.)* Come, ladies. We must be punctual or Costanza will take it as a sign that she too may be lax.

ROSE.  *(Taking a stand.)* Mrs. Graves.

MRS. GRAVES.  Yes?

ROSE.  About the sitting room.

MRS. GRAVES.  What?

LOTTY.  *(Smoothly.)* We are only too glad for you to have it, if it makes you happy, Mrs. Graves. We wouldn't have suggested using it had we known. *(Mrs. Graves tries to understand Lotty's intentions, decides not to bother, begins to exit into the villa.)* Not until you had invited us, anyhow. As I'm sure you soon shall. *(Mrs. Graves stops in disbelief.)*

MRS. GRAVES.  *(To Lotty.)* Do pull yourself together! *(She exits. Lotty sighs happily.)*

LOTTY.  We had so hoped to prepare things before your arrival, Lady Caroline.

CAROLINE.  Everything has been seen to.

LOTTY.  It must be very assuring to be independent, and to know exactly what one wants.

CAROLINE.  Quite.

ROSE.  *(Flatly.)* But independence, Lady Caroline, does snub the

34

benevolences of others.

CAROLINE. I'm sorry about the beds. I gave no directions. I merely asked Costanza to remove them.

LOTTY. *(Looking out.)* It seems silly to be talking about beds in heaven.

CAROLINE. It is lovely, isn't it?

LOTTY. It's as if you belonged here all along.

CAROLINE. What do you mean?

LOTTY. In a setting as beautiful as yourself. *(Caroline smiles. Rose frowns.)*

ROSE. Beauty is a gift.

CAROLINE. Yes.

ROSE. I hope you make the most of it, Lady Caroline.

CAROLINE. I've been making the most of it ever since I can remember.

ROSE. Good. Because it won't last. *(Caroline quiets, looks down, rises.)*

CAROLINE. Please tell Mrs. Graves that I don't care to take breakfast now. I'd like to go into the village. *(She starts to exit into the garden.)*

LOTTY. *(A little hurt.)* Oh. Hurry back, then.

CAROLINE. *(Stopping. To Lotty.)* I am glad you've arrived safely. *(She exits. Rose watches after her. Lotty looks around.)*

LOTTY. Oh, Rose. We haven't been punished. We've been blessed!

ROSE. She's treading on the periwinkles.

LOTTY. They're hers as much as ours.

ROSE. It doesn't seem right.

LOTTY. One mustn't question in heaven. It isn't done.

ROSE. We've been displaced as hostesses.

LOTTY. None of us is the hostess. Here we are equal. *(She closes her eyes and takes a deep breath.)* Smell the fragrance, Rose. It's positively … sensual!

ROSE. Lotty!

LOTTY. It makes me want to kiss someone! *(Lotty takes Rose's hand and kisses it.)* You know who would love all of this?

ROSE. Who? *(Lotty thinks, frowns.)*

LOTTY. Never mind. *(From within the house, the sound of Mrs. Graves furiously ringing her bell. The ladies shudder.)*

ROSE. That woman!

LOTTY. Mrs. Graves doesn't know yet that she's in heaven. Oh, take it in, Rose! *(Shouting to the skies.)* Paradiso! *(To Rose, beaming.)*

Our first day in heaven! *(Mrs. Graves' bell rings.)* And Gabriel here to greet us! *(She runs into the villa.)* Paradiso! *(Rose looks out, uncertain. She says a tiny prayer, closes her eyes and takes a deep, sensual breath. Something within her stirs. For the first time, she truly smiles. The church bell rings. Lights down.)*

## Scene 2

*Lights up on the terrace at San Salvatore, nine days later. Towels thrown about. Mrs. Graves sits at the table, hatless, face to the sun, sleeping. Costanza enters from the villa with a tray of tea and unshelled nuts, humming a tune gaily.*

COSTANZA.   *Buon giorno, Signora Graves. ("Good day." Mrs. Graves doesn't hear. Costanza continues to hum, and then suddenly shouts.)* Tè?! *("Tea?!")*
MRS. GRAVES.   *(Jumping.)* Ah! Yes! Yes. *(Opens her parasol and composes herself.)* Have you found the cracker yet?
COSTANZA.   *(Serving tea.)* "Cracker," *Signora?*
MRS. GRAVES.   The nutcracker. For the nuts.
COSTANZA.   *(Nodding.)* Ah, *sì, sì,* "thee cracker." No. *(Offering milk. Teasingly.)* Latte?
MRS. GRAVES.   *(With great patience.)* Thank you. *(Costanza pours.)*
COSTANZA.   *(Like a goat.)* Meh-eh-eh-eh-eh. *(She exits. Mrs. Graves eyes the tea with suspicion. Caroline enters, sees Mrs. Graves, tries to exit again, but is caught.)*
MRS. GRAVES.   Ah! Lady Caroline. There is tea if you like. More than a week now and it's still the only thing Costanza appears capable of preparing. There hasn't been a meal served yet that did not present some sort of primitive challenge. Although I am not at all certain why I bother. I am the only one in this party who arrives promptly for meals. Or arrives at all, for that matter. I spent breakfast quite alone.
CAROLINE.   *(Taking tea.)* That must have given you plenty of time to sit and remember.
MRS. GRAVES.   Remembrance and digestion should never be performed simultaneously. *(Rose enters. Her appearance has changed*

36

*considerably. She is dressed in a white summer dress, with her hair down, tied in the back. But she has been crying.)*
ROSE. Ladies.
CAROLINE. Hello.
MRS. GRAVES. Ah, Mrs. Arnott. You neglected breakfast.
ROSE. Have you seen Mrs. Wilton, Lady Caroline?
CAROLINE. Yes. She took the boat out.
MRS. GRAVES. Took the boat?
CAROLINE. The small rowing boat. She has quite a strong arm, our Lotty. *(Rose eyes Caroline.)*
MRS. GRAVES. Of that I have no doubt.
CAROLINE. *(To Rose.)* Are you all right?
ROSE. All of these flowers make my eyes water a little.
MRS. GRAVES. *(To Rose.)* That is a lovely frock you're wearing.
ROSE. *(Sighing cynically.)* Except for what, Mrs. Graves?
MRS. GRAVES. Sorry?
ROSE. You've nothing more to add?
MRS. GRAVES. No. Why?
CAROLINE. You've just complimented someone, Mrs. Graves.
MRS. GRAVES. *(Dumbfounded.)* Oh. *(Lotty enters from the garden in a swimming outfit, barefooted, breathless, beaming. She has gone wild from head to toe, flowers in hand and in her flowing hair.)*
LOTTY. Good day, everyone!
ROSE. Hello, Lotty.
MRS. GRAVES. Good Lord.
CAROLINE. Lotty! You look brilliant!
LOTTY. I feel brilliant, Lady Caroline! This has been the most glorious morning! Mrs. Graves, doesn't it all just make you want to burst?
MRS. GRAVES. I have never had a desire to burst.
LOTTY. *(Drying herself with a towel.)* I am famished! Is luncheon nearly ready?
ROSE. I believe so.
MRS. GRAVES. Not macaroni again?
ROSE. Yes.
MRS. GRAVES. *(With disdainful regret.)* From the land of Donatello.
LOTTY. Will you be joining us for luncheon today, Lady Caroline?
CAROLINE. *(Visibly annoyed that she is now surrounded.)* No, thank you. *(She begins to exit into the villa.)* I ... I've a touch of headache. Excuse me. *(She exits.)*
ROSE. What is the Italian for aspirin? *(She gets her phrase book.)*
MRS. GRAVES. The remedy for headache is castor oil.

LOTTY. She has no headache.

MRS. GRAVES. Carlyle suffered at one point terribly from headache ...

LOTTY. She has no headache. She only wants to be left alone.

MRS. GRAVES. Something else you've "seen," Mrs. Wilton?

LOTTY. Yes. When I looked at her just now, I saw inside of her.

MRS. GRAVES. I think I may burst after all.

LOTTY. *San Salvatore* is working its charms on Lady Caroline. *(Sneaking up behind Mrs. Graves and placing a flower in her hair, which Mrs. Graves doesn't notice.)* It's working its charms on all of us. Just at different rates, that's all. You really must take the boat out. Both of you. I've never felt so calm, or been able to think so clearly.

MRS. GRAVES. I think quite clearly enough, thank you.

LOTTY. And I've never wept so. A boat is a lovely place for weeping. *(Mrs. Graves has had enough.)*

MRS. GRAVES. *(Rising.)* I've castor oil in my room. *(She starts to exit.)* Mrs. Wilton, if you were a woman of greater age, your behavior could be understood as dotage. *(Lotty considers.)*

LOTTY. Well, if I did have a choice, Mrs. Graves, I suppose I would prefer dotage to condescension. *(Mrs. Graves stops, glares.)*

MRS. GRAVES. Cover your legs! *(She exits.)*

LOTTY. *(Inhales, looks about.)* Isn't it gorgeous to be part of this all, Rose? The dandelions and the lilies, me and Mrs. Graves ... all let in, all welcome!

ROSE. *(At wit's end.)* Honestly, Lotty. You'd make Pollyanna ill.

LOTTY. I can't help it. For the first time I feel such a part of everything!

ROSE. And what about me?

LOTTY. You must open yourself to it, Rose. You're angry.

ROSE. *(Strongly.)* Yes. I am.

LOTTY. That's good!

ROSE. You're all so independent.

LOTTY. Perhaps you don't want to be independent.

ROSE. I do!

LOTTY. Nine days without husbands. Perhaps that doesn't suit you, Rose. I have a confession myself. Since we arrived here there hasn't been one moment when I wasn't thinking of Mellersh.

ROSE. I dreamed of him last night.

LOTTY. Mellersh?

ROSE. Frederick.

LOTTY. "Frederick." So that's his name!

38

ROSE. And I forgot to say my prayers.

LOTTY. Your dream was your prayer.

ROSE. *That* ... is not what one prays for.

LOTTY. Physical love, you mean?

ROSE. Lotty! Mrs. Graves is right. Sometimes you are too much.

LOTTY. I can't help it, Rose. I don't know how else to be.

ROSE. It's selfish.

LOTTY. I am a particular challenge. As much as Mrs. Graves. And as much as poor Mellersh.

ROSE. Poor Mellersh? Are you hearing yourself?

LOTTY. Yes, I hear myself. Waking every morning to that second bed staring at me. I've been a miser, Rose. Rationing my love.

ROSE. What are you saying?

LOTTY. We must forgive our husbands, and ourselves, and get on with things.

ROSE. Lotty ... *(Lotty takes a deep breath.)*

LOTTY. I've written to Mellersh and told him everything.

ROSE. What?!

LOTTY. Well, except about my nest egg. I wish he were here so I could tell him that as well.

ROSE. You don't mean that.

LOTTY. I do, Rose. *(Nervously.)* I've ... invited him.

ROSE. *(Stunned.)* You can't be serious.

LOTTY. We said in London that there would be room for guests.

ROSE. We said in London that there would be an extra room.

LOTTY. *(Becoming increasingly excited.)* And there is! There's room for everyone! Even your Frederick.

ROSE. Frederick?

LOTTY. Do you call him "Freddy"?

ROSE. I do not. *(Becoming increasingly upset.)* The whole idea of our coming here was to get away.

LOTTY. We got away!

ROSE. And now, after barely one week of it, you want to ask the very people ...

LOTTY. The very people we were getting away from. It's true. It's idiotically illogical. But they must be here now. I've seen it!

ROSE. Stop this, Lotty. I'm warning you.

LOTTY. Write to your Frederick, Rose, and tell him everything!

ROSE. It's not that simple.

LOTTY. About *San Salvatore* ... and the wisteria ...

ROSE. You can't understand ... *(Lotty laughs.)*

LOTTY. And Mrs. Graves, and …

ROSE. *(Desperately.)* LISTEN TO ME! He wouldn't come!

LOTTY. Don't be silly.

ROSE. I lost a child, Lotty. I lost my child. Our child.

LOTTY. *(Quietly.)* Oh, Rose.

ROSE. Our beauty. It's been four years now, but …

LOTTY. No …

ROSE. Four years of trying to understand such a … punishment.

LOTTY. *(Going to Rose, holding her.)* No. No. *(Rose embraces her, crying.)* Rose. *(Thinks.)* I can't pretend to know what you're feeling, Rose. But I do know that you are not alone.

ROSE. I have you now.

LOTTY. Not me. Frederick.

ROSE. You're not listening.

LOTTY. You must invite him.

ROSE. He won't come.

LOTTY. He will. I've seen it! Frederick and Mellersh. At *San Salvatore. (Rose smiles.)*

ROSE. How can you see Frederick, Lotty? You don't know a thing about him.

LOTTY. You're such a damned logical woman, Mrs. Arnott. *(Lotty extends her hand.)* Come. Let me take you boating. You can tell me everything.

ROSE. You said you were hungry.

LOTTY. We'll pick berries. You're right, Rose. I haven't been listening. But we're sisters, remember? And I'm listening now. *(Rose takes Lotty's hand. They exit into the garden. Caroline enters from the villa, sees them leaving, sighs, relieved. She goes to the chaise, retrieves a flask from behind the pillows, opens it, drinks, exhales deeply. Mrs. Graves enters from the villa, flower in hair and castor oil in hand. She watches Caroline replace the flask.)*

MRS. GRAVES. Castor oil! *(Caroline smoothes herself.)* I expect the sun has caused you to feel ill. You should take some castor oil and go to bed.

CAROLINE. But I don't want castor oil, and I don't want to go to bed. I just want to be alone to think.

MRS. GRAVES. No one wants a woman who thinks. You should go to bed and get well.

CAROLINE. I am well.

MRS. GRAVES. Then I have had all the trouble of coming after you for nothing.

CAROLINE. Wouldn't you prefer coming after me and finding me well to coming after me and finding me ill? *(Mrs. Graves lets out a small laugh, walks into the sun and looks up, inhales deeply. Costanza enters with a telegram.)*

COSTANZA. *Un telegramma, per la Signora Wilton. ("A telegram, for Mrs. Wilton.")*

CAROLINE. *È nel giardino, Costanza. ("She is in the garden.")*

COSTANZA. *Ah. Grazie, Donna Carolina. (She exits into the garden, calling.) Signora Wilton! Un telegramma! Signora Wilton!*

MRS. GRAVES. Now who could be sending Mrs. Wilton a telegram?

CAROLINE. You shouldn't be so hard on Lotty, Mrs. Graves.

MRS. GRAVES. That woman must be curbed.

CAROLINE. She understands things, I think, in her way.

MRS. GRAVES. She "sees" things, you mean. Just a moment ago she said she saw inside of you.

CAROLINE. If that's so, then she's one of the few people who has ever bothered. *(Mrs. Graves considers.)*

MRS. GRAVES. You are an intriguing creature, Lady Caroline. I am very glad there are no men about. You are precisely the sort of woman who unbalances men. My mother unbalanced men, and I dare say it can come at quite a cost.

CAROLINE. Pricey, was she? *(Mrs. Graves glares.)* I apologize, Mrs. Graves. Sometimes I can go too far.

MRS. GRAVES. I understand some things myself, Lady Caroline, in my way. The burden of wit on our sex, for example. You should be thankful for your beauty. At least you are allowed credit for that.

CAROLINE. I would gladly trade it all, Mrs. Graves.

MRS. GRAVES. *(Chuckling.)* For what?

CAROLINE. Things lost.

MRS. GRAVES. How so?

CAROLINE. Jolly war, wasn't it? Except for those who never returned. And those of us who loved them. *(Mrs. Graves softens.)*

MRS. GRAVES. A brother?

CAROLINE. Never mind.

MRS. GRAVES. You are impossible.

CAROLINE. A husband.

MRS. GRAVES. A husband? I ... *(Moved.)* I am sorry ... I didn't know.

CAROLINE. No one did. We secretly married the night before his duty. For good luck. Funny, no?

MRS. GRAVES.  I … I am very surprised you've told me this, Lady Caroline.

CAROLINE.  You have such a warm way of drawing people in, Mrs. Graves.

MRS. GRAVES.  I grieved terribly when I lost my Clayton. That came as quite a surprise, I must say. Not nearly as surprising as it would have been to him.

CAROLINE.  I had a reputation to uphold. I danced instead.

MRS. GRAVES.  You've not found another?

CAROLINE.  Another? We are the "moderns" now, Mrs. Graves. There's always another. When the wine has been spilt, there's still the dregs. Artists who want to "mold" me, photographers who want to "capture" me. And writers … well, what woman wouldn't want to be studied, annotated, indexed?

MRS. GRAVES.  They adore you, I'm sure.

CAROLINE.  They don't even know me.

MRS. GRAVES.  Are you certain that's their fault? *(Caroline softens.)*

CAROLINE.  To be fair, there is one. Are you familiar with Florian Ayers? *(Mrs. Graves shudders.)*

MRS. GRAVES.  Florian Ayers? That writer?!

CAROLINE.  Mother's latest social acquisition.

MRS. GRAVES.  "Romantic biographies."

CAROLINE.  Indeed.

MRS. GRAVES.  Salacious!

CAROLINE.  And wildly successful.

MRS. GRAVES.  Good God. *(Thinks.)* I once had a dog that chased his own tail.

CAROLINE.  And?

MRS. GRAVES.  People praised him, too.

CAROLINE.  But Florian is sweet, really. And sad somehow. A lost soulmate, perhaps. *(Mrs. Graves thinks, stirred.)*

MRS. GRAVES.  A lost soulmate. I feel so restless today.

CAROLINE.  You've gotten some sun, Mrs. Graves. *(Mrs. Graves retrieves her parasol, starts to open it.)* It becomes you. *(Mrs. Graves smiles, closes the parasol. Lotty lets out a great yelp from the garden.)*

LOTTY.  *(Offstage.)* Mrs. Graves! Lady Caroline!

MRS. GRAVES.  Lady Caroline. About the cognac.

LOTTY.  *(Offstage.)* Paradiso!

MRS. GRAVES.  Don't trade everything for that. *(Lotty enters from the garden excitedly, with Rose and Costanza, who have been dressed in flowers.)*

LOTTY. *Paradiso,* Lady Caroline! *Paradiso,* Mrs. Graves!

MRS. GRAVES. Good God!

LOTTY. Ladies. Ladies.

CAROLINE. What is it, Lotty?

LOTTY. It's wonderful, that's what it is! I'm sorry that this is without warning, but ... I am having a visitor!

MRS. GRAVES. What?!

CAROLINE. But we came here to escape people, Lotty.

LOTTY. Yes, I know. But I don't want to escape him now.

CAROLINE. Him?

MRS. GRAVES. A man?!

LOTTY. Yes, a man. Mr. Wilton!

MRS. GRAVES. A relative?

LOTTY. A husband!

MRS. GRAVES. Mrs. Wilton, if this is another one of your ghosts ...

LOTTY. No, Mrs. Graves. It's my husband! In the flesh! *(Lifting the telegram.)* He left London last night!

MRS. GRAVES. But you are a widow!

ROSE. She never said anything of the kind, Mrs. Graves.

LOTTY. Lady Caroline, I'll need your help with Costanza to prepare the spare room and then ...

MRS. GRAVES. *(Increasingly irate.)* One moment! Am I to understand that you are proposing to reserve the one unoccupied bedroom in the castle for the exclusive use of your family?

CAROLINE. Yes, why the spare room if he's your husband, Lotty?

LOTTY. Oh, no. If I share my room with Mellersh, I risk losing all I'm feeling. Don't you see?

CAROLINE. *(Laughing.)* Actually, I do! By all means, let's give Mr. Wilton the spare room, Mrs. Graves. Any other arrangement would be scandalous!

LOTTY. Thank you, Caroline. And Rose is going to write to her husband.

MRS. GRAVES. Another husband?!

LOTTY. Aren't you, Rose?

ROSE. Yes. I am!

MRS. GRAVES. Is anyone here who they claimed to be?

CAROLINE. But there is only one spare room.

LOTTY. Oh, Rose won't mind sharing her room with her husband. It's written all over her. *(Rose gasps, tries to grab Lotty, but she runs. Caroline laughs.)*

MRS. GRAVES. Husbands were not part of our agreement, Mrs.

Arnott. You must not write to him.

ROSE. As you wish, Mrs. Graves. *(Gathering strength.)* I'll telegraph him!

MRS. GRAVES. Oh! Well … I am going to invite a guest!

ROSE. Who, Mrs. Graves? Tennyson or Carlyle? *(Lotty gasps. Mrs. Graves boils.)*

MRS. GRAVES. I have a friend! Kate Lumley! *(The ladies laugh.)* Oh, the laughter will end when Kate Lumley arrives, I assure you. I shall write to her this instant, and she will have the spare room! There are to be no men roaming *San Salvatore* as long as I am staying here. Kate Lumley will see to that! *(Wilding enters from the villa.)*

WILDING. Cheers, everyone!

MRS. GRAVES. *(Appalled.)* Oh!

LOTTY. *(Thrilled.)* Mr. Wilding!

WILDING. Is this a bad time? I was passing through to Rome and thought I'd see how things were going.

LOTTY. This is too much!

MRS. GRAVES. I should say! *(She rings her bell furiously, sits.)*

CAROLINE. *(Noticeably impressed.)* You may remember my letter, Mr. Wilding. *(Lifts her hand.)* Lady Caroline Bramble. *(Wilding nods, looks to Rose excitedly.)*

WILDING. Mrs. Arnott! *(He goes to Rose, takes her hand, spins her around.)* And you wore white!

ROSE. *(Beaming.)* Mr. Wilding!

WILDING. It's just as I saw it!

LOTTY. It's just as *I* saw it! *(Costanza enters, sees Wilding.)*

COSTANZA. *Tonio! (She runs to Wilding. They embrace.)*

WILDING. *Costanza!*

COSTANZA. *Bambino mio! ("My little boy!")*

MRS. GRAVES. Oh, good God!

COSTANZA. *(To Wilding, pointing at Mrs. Graves.) Pazza! (Miming horns.) Diabolica! ("Crazy! Diabolical!")*

WILDING. All my ladies!

CAROLINE. *(Snubbed.)* Well.

WILDING. At *San Salvatore*!

MRS. GRAVES. Really!

WILDING. And this must be the Mrs. Graves you told me of …

MRS. GRAVES. *(Furiously.)* Mr. Wilding!

WILDING. For whom I've carried, all the way from London, a bag of the finest English walnuts … *(He kneels before Mrs. Graves,*

*holding out a ribboned bag. Mrs. Graves' eyes widen.)* ... which I shall gladly trade for a few hours in your lovely company, and the promise of hearing your golden memories of the great Lord Tennyson. *(Mrs. Graves opens her mouth, but is wordless, dazed. She reaches daintily for the bag, a coquettish grin spreading slowly across her face.)*
MRS. GRAVES. *(Bubbling over.)* Make yourself at home! *(Lights down.)*


# Scene 3


*Lights up on the terrace of San Salvatore, the following afternoon. Rose sits on the chaise in her white dress, hair loose, with parasol, posing for Wilding, who stands before a canvas and easel, sketching her.*


WILDING. That's it. And just a little ... there. Would you lift your chin just a ... *(She does so.)* Yes. You have a fine chin, Mrs. Arnott. And now it is ... caught. I must say you have shown admirable patience.
ROSE. I hope that won't be the tone of the portrait, Mr. Wilding.
WILDING. Oh?
ROSE. I should hate to one day find myself used in textbooks as an illustration of "admirable patience." *(Costanza enters from the villa with tea.)*
COSTANZA. *Tè.*
WILDING. *(Not looking up from his work.)* Grazie, Costanza. *(Costanza sees Rose.)*
COSTANZA. *Ah! Squisita! Bellissima! ("Lovely! Beautiful!")*
ROSE. Is that good?
WILDING. Quite. *(Costanza looks at the sketch.)*
COSTANZA. *Oh, Tonio. Meravigliosa! ("Marvelous!")*
WILDING. *Vi ricorda qualcuno, Costanza? ("Does she remind you of anyone?")*
COSTANZA. *Mi ricorda? ("Remind me?" Thinks, realizes, sadly.) Ah, sì. Lo vedo. ("Yes, I see it." Changing the subject.) Ma quando dipingerai il ritratto di Costanza? ("But when are you going to paint Costanza's portrait?" She poses.)*

WILDING. *Ho già fatto! Troppo difettoso non posso mostrarlo in pubblico. ("I have! Too bad I can't show them in public.")*

COSTANZA. Eh? *(Realizes he's teasing, laughs, embarrassed.)* Oh tu! *Diavolino! Tu sei il figlio del tuo papa, non c'è dubbio! ("Oh, you! Little devil! You are your father's boy, no doubt about it!" Wagging her finger as she exits into the villa.) Sei il figlio di papa!*

ROSE. *(Still posing.)* Costanza is very fond of you.

WILDING. Oh, yes. Part of the family. Part of *her* family, I mean. Costanza is the mother of nine.

ROSE. Nine?!

WILDING. Ten, counting me now, I suppose.

ROSE. Speaking of admirable patience.

WILDING. I owe Costanza a great deal. She was wonderful with Mother. Here … you've worked enough. Let's have some tea. *(Wilding pours tea and prepares a small plate of biscuits. Rose stands, stretches. She's unusually relaxed. She motions toward the sketch.)*

ROSE. May I?

WILDING. Of course. *(She takes a look.)* Mind you, it's only a sketch.

ROSE. *(Moved.)* It's lovely, Mr. Wilding.

WILDING. I shall finish it properly in Rome. *(Rose smiles, walks to the tea.)*

ROSE. Rome must be fascinating.

WILDING. *(Handing her a cup of tea.)* Very beautiful. Very romantic. And one must have one's escape, mustn't one? *(They are close. Rose smells the tea.)*

ROSE. Cinnamon.

WILDING. *"Cannella."*

ROSE. *Cannella.*

WILDING. *Sì.* Biscotto? *(He offers her the plate of biscuits.)*

ROSE. *(Blushing.)* Grazie. *(She takes the plate, sits.)* Is Mrs. Wilton still out?

WILDING. Yes. Well, out again, that is. She and Mrs. Graves went to the village.

ROSE. To the village? Mrs. Graves?

WILDING. Does that surprise you?

ROSE. I suppose yesterday it would have. But since you've arrived, Mr. Wilding, we seem to have a somewhat altered Mrs. Graves.

WILDING. Really? I find her most delightful.

ROSE. You've doted on her properly. You've doted on us all.

WILDING. Sometimes all it takes is a little attention to do the trick. *(He sits next to Rose.)* You must admit, Mrs. Arnott, that I was correct about something.

ROSE. What?

WILDING. That you were meant to be at *San Salvatore.*

ROSE. *(Thoroughly, pleasantly embarrassed.)* You and Costanza just now ...

WILDING. Yes?

ROSE. Were you comparing me with the original? *(Wilding is stunned.)*

WILDING. The ... what? *(Rose senses she's said something wrong.)*

ROSE. The portrait of the Madonna? Above the stairs?

WILDING. *(Relieved.)* Oh. Yes. You have to admit the likeness is extraordinary.

ROSE. I didn't know I looked so solemn.

WILDING. You don't. Not today.

ROSE. I don't think my vicar would approve of such comparisons.

WILDING. No, no. But then that's what vicars do, don't they? *(Rose smiles. Wilding looks at her.)* Actually, it's someone else you remind me of.

ROSE. Not some "old flame," I pray.

WILDING. Oh, no, no. Nothing of that nature. *(Wilding thinks. Rose becomes a little uncertain, but smiles inquisitively.)* There are moments, Mrs. Arnott, when you remind me so much of my mother. *(Total silence. Rose keeps her composure. Except for the biscuits, which spill from her plate to the floor.)*

ROSE. *(Rising.)* Oh!

WILDING. Oh, dear. *(He takes the plate, retrieves the biscuits.)* Here, I'll get you more.

ROSE. No, no. *(She looks out as Wilding busies with the biscuits, catches her breath, thinks.)* I know you were very close to your mother, Mr. Wilding. So it's very nice of you to say such a thing.

WILDING. I saw it the first time we met.

ROSE. I see. Are there any photographs of her here?

WILDING. I wish there were. Mother was much too modest for that. Father and I both tried, but she'd have none of it, I'm afraid.

ROSE. And what was your father like, Mr. Wilding?

WILDING. Father? Father loved beauty. He loved life. He lived life. Mother was always a little embarrassed by that, I think. A shame, really. Because she *was* his life. He flat out adored her.

ROSE. Sweet.

WILDING. *(Looking out, pointing.)* Do you see that acacia tree there? *(Rose looks out.)* Father told a story that his father, my grand-father, while walking one day with my grandmother, thrust his walking stick into the ground at that spot and said, "Here we shall have an acacia." He left the stick in the ground as a reminder, and presently, how long afterward nobody seems to remember, the stick began to sprout. And it was an acacia. *(Rose smiles.)* After duty, in hospital, I tried to paint that tree, but could never do it justice.

ROSE. Were you wounded?

WILDING. Just … a bit tired. I came straight from hospital to *San Salvatore*, in fact. And Mother and Costanza.

ROSE. I'm sure that cured you. *(Wilding smiles, sadly. Lotty yells from the garden.)*

LOTTY. *(Offstage.)* Yoo Hoo!

WILDING. Here they are.

ROSE. They look as if they've bought the whole place! *(Lotty enters from the garden with Mrs. Graves on her arm. Mrs. Graves' mode of dress has lightened. Lotty is bright and well-groomed. They are laden with packages, with which Wilding helps.)*

LOTTY. We're almost there, Mrs. Graves.

MRS. GRAVES. Good God, you've been saying that for an hour.

LOTTY. And now it's true! Thank you, Mr. Wilding.

WILDING. I should have gone along, ladies.

LOTTY. Oh, no. We made much progress on our own, didn't we, Mrs. Graves?

MRS. GRAVES. We march on Rome tomorrow.

LOTTY. We are in for a treat, everyone!

MRS. GRAVES. Well, I make no promises, but I have at least pro-cured the makings of a proper meal. Tonight I shall teach Costanza how to prepare steak and kidney pie.

LOTTY. Rose, perhaps you'd help me with Costanza. There's teaching to be done!

ROSE. Yes. *(Lotty and Rose gather the packages.)*

WILDING. Shall I have Costanza bring tea inside?

MRS. GRAVES. *(Sweetly.)* I should like to take my tea out here with you, Mr. Wilding.

WILDING. Very well.

LOTTY. Thank you for a grand time, Mrs. Graves. *(She kisses Mrs. Graves on the cheek, exits. Mrs. Graves is aghast.)*

ROSE. And thank *you*, Mr. Wilding. For everything.

WILDING. I haven't done anything, Mrs. Arnott.

ROSE. *(Sincerely.)* You have. *(She exits.)*

MRS. GRAVES. Mr. Wilding. I would like tonight's dinner to be my thanks for your generous company. I am sorry you are leaving tomorrow. It is so nice to have a man about the place.

WILDING. I'm glad *San Salvatore* agrees with you, Mrs. Graves.

MRS. GRAVES. How could it not? You are very young to be a man of property.

WILDING. I can hardly take credit for that.

MRS. GRAVES. But you should. Inheritance is so much more respectable than acquisition.

WILDING. How did you fare in the village?

MRS. GRAVES. Oh, that Mrs. Wilton is a stubborn thing. From day one I have tried to make peace with her, but to no avail.

WILDING. With some people there seems to be no choice but to relent.

MRS. GRAVES. No! To relent is to surrender, Mr. Wilding. That is not the English way at all. You have spent far too much time in Italy, I fear. *(She walks to the sketch.)*

WILDING. Perhaps you are right.

MRS. GRAVES. This Mrs. Arnott is a particular case herself.

WILDING. Yes.

MRS. GRAVES. *(Watching his reaction.)* Yes. Tell me, Mr. Wilding, what do you make of our Lady Caroline?

WILDING. She's lovely. I seem to have made a poor impression, however.

MRS. GRAVES. There's more to Lady Caroline than meets the eye.

WILDING. She is very solitary.

MRS. GRAVES. A common thing today, it seems, since the war.

WILDING. And you? I picture you in London surrounded by grandchildren.

MRS. GRAVES. Grand...? Oh no, no. One needs children to have grandchildren, Mr. Wilding. *(Caroline enters.)*

WILDING. Ah! Lady Caroline.

MRS. GRAVES. Who missed dinner again last night.

CAROLINE. I wasn't feeling well.

WILDING. I do hope you are feeling better.

MRS. GRAVES. Our Lady Caroline has a remarkable inclination toward rapid recovery. *(She sits and places her stick aside.)*

CAROLINE. Mr. Wilding. Since you are here, perhaps something can be done about the bath. It is really quite a confusion.

WILDING. *(Cordially.)* A confusion?

CAROLINE. One shouldn't have to risk one's life merely for the convenience of warm water.

WILDING. *(Chuckling.)* Oh yes, the heater. It is a rather ancient system. But really, there is no danger at all if done with just a little Italian patience. *(He and Mrs. Graves smile.)*

CAROLINE. *(Coldly.)* It is a danger, Mr. Wilding. Am I understood? *(Wilding realizes he has misspoken.)*

WILDING. I shall look into the matter before my departure. *(Costanza enters from the villa, upset.)*

COSTANZA. Signora Graves?

MRS. GRAVES. Ah! I am needed! *(She rises and heads toward the villa.)*

COSTANZA. *(Pleadingly.)* Tonio?

WILDING. *(Seeing Costanza's distress.)* Sì, sì, Costanza. May I be of some help, Mrs. Graves?

MRS. GRAVES. Well … you could lure Mrs. Wilton out here, so that I need not contend with her in the kitchen.

CAROLINE. Mrs. Graves? *(Mrs. Graves stops. Slyly.)* Your stick. *(Mrs. Graves and Wilding look at the stick, which has been left behind.)*

MRS. GRAVES. *(Flustered.)* Well. *(Wilding retrieves the stick, hands it to her.)* Imagine that. *(She exits into the villa.)*

WILDING. Lady Caroline, I am sorry about the bath. I do hope you'll join us this evening for dinner.

CAROLINE. *(Flatly.)* Do you?

WILDING. I do. Excuse me. *(He exits into the villa. Costanza enters and approaches Caroline, holds out a card.)*

COSTANZA. Un biglietto da visita, Donna Carolina. *("A visitor's card.")*

CAROLINE. Che? *("What?" Reads the card, gasps.)* Good God! *(Laughs.)*

COSTANZA. È nell'entrata. *("He is in the entry way.")*

CAROLINE. Portalo qui, per favore, Costanza. *("Bring him out, please.")*

COSTANZA. Sì, sì, Signorina. *(Exits into the villa. Caroline readies herself.)*

CAROLINE. Well, now. *(Costanza enters with Frederick. Caroline turns on her charms.)* Florian Ayers!

FREDERICK. Ah! Caroline! I had no idea if I was at the right place.

CAROLINE. You naughty boy!

FREDERICK. *(With uncertain joviality.)* Your mother told me where you were, and I was on my book tour anyhow, and so I thought I would look in and see how you were doing.

CAROLINE. I don't recall your book tour extending to Italy.

FREDERICK. Yes, well. It doesn't really. *(Weakly.)* But I was already in Lisbon ...

CAROLINE. You are a wicked thing, Mr. Ayers.

FREDERICK. No, no. Just weak, I'm told.

CAROLINE. Didn't mother tell you I was doing a rest cure?

FREDERICK. Yes, she did. That's why I haven't intruded on you earlier in the day. I thought you would probably sleep all day and get up just in time for tea. *(Crumbling.)* I couldn't help myself, Caroline. *(Costanza clears her throat.)*

CAROLINE. *Grazie, Costanza.*

COSTANZA. *(Skeptically.) Uno in più per cena? ("One more for dinner?")*

CAROLINE. *Sì. Grazie. (Costanza exits into the villa.)*

FREDERICK. What did you say?

CAROLINE. I told her to add you to dinner. *(Finding it difficult to maintain her carefree pose.)* Mother didn't send you, did she, Florian?

FREDERICK. Oh no, on my word, Caroline.

CAROLINE. I wanted to have a month that was perfectly blank.

FREDERICK. And now I've interrupted.

CAROLINE. *(Sincerely.)* I feel all a jumble.

FREDERICK. *(Attempting again to lift the mood.)* Perhaps it's good I came then! There's a jazz club in Genoa! I was given the name. Something "Eeny," "Leeny," "Cheeny." I'm told it's quite the thing!

CAROLINE. I'm so tired, Florian.

FREDERICK. *(Uncomfortably.) You*, Caroline? *(Seeing the sketch, deflecting.)* Have you taken up art now? *(He goes to the sketch, studies it, at first with pleasure, and then with utter bewilderment.)*

CAROLINE. I don't know what to do anymore.

FREDERICK. *(Scratching his head, transfixed.)* Nothing a little jazz and gin won't cure, is there? Speaking of which ... *(Turning back to Caroline, dazed.)* I seem to be a little dry at the moment. Any "refreshments" hereabout?

CAROLINE. There's tea.

FREDERICK. *(Disappointed.)* Oh.

CAROLINE. Here. *(She retrieves the flask.)* This will help.

FREDERICK. There's my girl. *(He drinks, glances toward the sketch. Caroline thinks.)*

CAROLINE. *(Sadly.)* Florian? Have you ever lost hold of something? Something so vital that you didn't know how to go on?

*(Frederick considers.)*
FREDERICK. *(Sincerely.)* I have.
CAROLINE. What did you do?
FREDERICK. I went on.
CAROLINE. But it's not the same.
FREDERICK. No.
CAROLINE. You've always seemed like someone I could talk to, Florian. There's something disarmingly… *honest* about you.
FREDERICK. *(Dropping all pretense.)* We *should* talk, Caroline. Perhaps we can find a restaurant in the village.
CAROLINE. Yes? Oh, but there's to be a special dinner here tonight.
FREDERICK. We can make an early appearance and then go. Here. *(He hands her the flask. Caroline smiles, decides not to drink, closes the flask.)*
CAROLINE. *(Indicating the chaise.)* You lie down and rest a bit, then. Let me go change.
FREDERICK. I could do with a rest. *(Goes to the chaise.)* That's really quite a climb up from the village. There was a motorcar at the station, but the driver was too busy arguing with some other chap. So many English in Italy this time of year.
CAROLINE. Well, rest, and then you can regale all of us at dinner with stories of your tour.
FREDERICK. "All of us"? I hope I'm not interrupting anything.
CAROLINE. Ladies.
FREDERICK. Ah! *(Caroline starts to exit into the villa, stops.)*
CAROLINE. Tell me something. The jazz and the gin. Would you ever give it all up? *(Frederick thinks, sighs.)*
FREDERICK. Gladly. *(Caroline smiles, gives him a quick kiss, exits. Frederick looks around, relaxes back on the chaise, settles in, shuts his eyes, rests. Rose enters from the villa, goes to the sketch, studies it. Frederick begins singing "Ma, He's Making Eyes at Me" under his breath. Rose looks up, sees him, freezes in disbelief. She walks to him.)*
ROSE. Frederick?
FREDERICK. *(Dreaming.)* Rose.
ROSE. Frederick! *(Frederick opens his eyes, stares.)*
FREDERICK. Rose? *(He jumps up, amazed at her appearance, stunned by her presence.)* Rose! *(Rose throws her arms around him, kissing him passionately. Costanza enters, sees, crosses herself, exits.)*
ROSE. Frederick! Oh, Frederick! When did you start?
FREDERICK. *(Trying to decipher between kisses.)* Start?
ROSE. Yes. When did you leave?

FREDERICK. *(Attempting an acceptable answer, weakly.)* Yesterday morning?
ROSE. The very instant then!
FREDERICK. Yes! The very instant!
ROSE. How quickly my telegram must have got to Lisbon!
FREDERICK. *(Understanding.)* Telegram! Yes, yes, didn't it though!
ROSE. Oh, Frederick! Frederick! *(She kisses him fully. Wilding enters from the villa, sees.)*
WILDING. Well, I'm damned.
ROSE. Oh! Oh, Mr. Wilding! Mr. Wilding. Forgive me. I'm so embarrassed.
WILDING. No, no.
ROSE. *(To Frederick.)* This is Mr. Frederick, Wilding ... *(Laughs. To Wilding.)* Oh ... I mean, this is Mr. Arnott, Frederick. *(Laughs, composes herself.)* Mr. Wilding, this ... *(Smiles.)* ... is my husband ... *Mister* Arnott.
FREDERICK. How ... how do you do? *(They shake hands.)*
WILDING. I'm not quite sure, really.
ROSE. Mr. Wilding owns the castle, Frederick.
FREDERICK. *(Wide-eyed, ready to say anything.)* Ah! Beautiful!
WILDING. Yes.
ROSE. *(Giddily.)* Oh, Frederick. I didn't know whether to write or not, whether you wanted ... but Lotty made me believe!
FREDERICK. Oh, well, Lotty, yes. Who's Lotty?
ROSE. Lotty! Mrs. Wilton. One of the other guests. She's from Hampstead as well. And, oh, there's Mrs. Graves. I don't know what you'll make of her. And Lady Caroline Bramble!
FREDERICK. *(Weakly.)* Really? Lady Caroline Bramble?
WILDING. If you'll excuse me ...
ROSE. *(Choosing her words as discreetly as possible, trying to hide her excitement, gathering Frederick's things.)* Oh, no. If you'll be so kind to excuse *us*, Mr. Wilding, I think it would be best if Mr. Arnott and myself retired presently to our room to ... prepare for dinner.
WILDING. Right. Right, then. A pleasure meeting you, Mr. Arnott.
FREDERICK. Likewise.
ROSE. Oh, Frederick! *(Taking his hand and leading him toward the villa.)* Lotty always said we must believe that anything can happen. And it can!
FREDERICK. *(Flummoxed.)* Yes. Apparently it can! *(They exit. Costanza enters from the villa, holds out a card.)*
COSTANZA. *Tonio! Un altro!* *("Another.")*

WILDING. *Un altro? (He takes the card. A newly humbled Mellersh timidly enters from the villa, clutching his travel bag, hat, coat, and Italian phrase book.) Buon giorno.*

MELLERSH. *(Attempting Italian, badly.)* Bu-on gi-or-no. Par ... parla ... Ing ... Ing ... *("Do you speak English?")*

WILDING. *Inglese?* Not only do I speak English, I am English.

MELLERSH. Ah! Thank heavens! *(He hands his things to Costanza.)* Mellersh Wilton, family solicitor.

WILDING. So it says. Antony Wilding. *(They shake hands.)*

MELLERSH. How do you do?

WILDING. You are a relative of our Mrs. Wilton?

MELLERSH. You could say that. *(Looking about. Completely out of his element.)* Then my wife is here?

WILDING. *(Perplexed.)* Who?

MELLERSH. Mrs. Wilton.

WILDING. *(Stunned.)* Your wife?! Yes, yes. She's just in the kitchen with Mrs. Graves. *(To himself.)* Now she's a widow, surely. *(Composing himself.)* Costanza, prenda Signora Wilton, prego. *("Get Mrs. Wilton.")*

COSTANZA. *(At wit's end.)* Sì, Tonio. Quanti sono per cena adesso? *("How many for dinner now?")*

WILDING. *Sette. A meno che non ci aspettino altre sorprese. ("Seven. Unless there are even more surprises.")*

COSTANZA. *Sì, sì. È una sorpresa dopo l'altra! ("It's just one surprise after another!" She exits, pointedly leaving Mellersh's things.)*

WILDING. Costanza will fetch her for you. You look parched. Would you like some tea?

MELLERSH. Oh, please!

WILDING. *(Serving.)* Any trouble finding the place?

MELLERSH. A struggle or two, but I rallied.

WILDING. You're familiar with Italy?

MELLERSH. *(Weakly.)* I've read books. *(Takes the tea, drinks.)* Thank you. *(Assessing Wilding, uncomfortably.)* My wife wrote that this was a party of four ladies.

WILDING. Yes. *(Mellersh waits.)*

MELLERSH. And you?

WILDING. I suppose I'm what you'd call the landlord.

MELLERSH. You mean you are the owner of the place?

WILDING. Yes.

MELLERSH. Oh? *(Pleased.)* Oh! My wife also wrote that Lady Caroline Bramble was among the guests.

WILDING. Yes.

MELLERSH. *(Even more pleased.)* Well! *(Lotty enters from the villa.)*

LOTTY. *(Softly.)* Hello, Mellersh. *(Mellersh grins, turns, but turns away again and composes himself.)*

MELLERSH. Mrs. Wilton. *(A nervous moment. Lotty is ready to burst, and she does. She rushes toward Mellersh.)*

LOTTY. Oh, Mellersh! Welcome! *(Mellersh jumps. His tea cup flies from its saucer and is caught by Wilding.)*

MELLERSH. Good heavens, Charlotte!

LOTTY. Have you and Mr. Wilding introduced yourselves?

MELLERSH. Surely.

LOTTY. Are you all right, Mr. Wilding?

WILDING. *(Dazed.)* What? Oh, no … I mean yes! Fine, fine. *(He returns the cup to its saucer.)* I suppose I should go check on the steak and kidney pie. *(To himself, exiting.)* Widows!

LOTTY. I am so glad to see you, Mellersh!

MELLERSH. Really? But you couldn't meet me at the station?

LOTTY. Oh, but I had so much to do! And the time … well, *San Salvatore* has a way of making one forget all about time.

MELLERSH. *(Attempting control.)* Forget about time? Absurd.

LOTTY. It's not absurd. You'll see.

MELLERSH. I would like to pay my respects to your hostess, Charlotte.

LOTTY. Hostess?

MELLERSH. This "Mrs. Arnott" who invited you here.

LOTTY. There is something I haven't told you, Mellersh.

MELLERSH. There appear to be many things you haven't told me.

LOTTY. *(Nervously.)* I … wasn't invited here.

MELLERSH. Not…? You named three ladies in your telegram.

LOTTY. Yes. The four of us are here.

MELLERSH. And this Mr. Wilding.

LOTTY. I know it must seem confusing, Mellersh, and it should to you, and for that I do apologize. But, you see … it's just that the four of us ladies, we … well … we have rented the castle.

MELLERSH. Rented?

LOTTY. Yes. Together. Each of us is paying her own share.

MELLERSH. *(Aghast.)* Paying?! How much?

LOTTY. That, Mellersh … I'm afraid … is really not at all your affair. *(She gasps and covers her mouth. Mellersh's jaw drops.)* It came out of my dress allowance. My nest egg. I know you have every reason to be angry and hurt, Mellersh, but I hope you won't and will forgive me instead. This holiday has meant everything to me. Look at me! I've been translated!

MELLERSH. Trans…?

LOTTY. That's why I wanted you here. To be translated with me!

MELLERSH. You know my feelings about secrets, Charlotte!

LOTTY. I know, Mellersh.

MELLERSH. Secrets are like …

LOTTY. Rust.

MELLERSH. Yes!

LOTTY. *(Shouting.)* BUT LOOK AT ME! *(Mellersh looks, at last. Lotty is aglow.)* I'm not a bit rusty, now, am I? *(She goes to him, kisses him passionately. Mellersh is left breathless, blushing.)*

MELLERSH. Well! *(Shudders, turns away, feigning control.)* If I have made my point, then … I would very much like a hot bath.

LOTTY. *(Beaming.)* Yes, Mellersh, of course. Costanza!

MELLERSH. Exactly what is it I'm to be translated into, Charlotte?

LOTTY. Oh, you'll see, Mellersh. You'll see. *(Costanza enters from the villa.)*

COSTANZA. *(Wearily.)* Sì, Signora?

LOTTY. Ah, Costanza. *Signore* Wilton … *(Smiling.)* … my husband, Costanza … *Signore* Wilton wants a hot bath. Bath. *(Costanza stares blankly.)*

MELLERSH. The Italian for bath is *"bag-no,"* my dear. *Bag-no.* Here, let me attend to it. *(His Italian is comically overdramatic and poorly pronounced.)* Io vo-gli-o un bag-no cal-do. *("I would like a hot bath." Costanza continues to stare.)* Are you certain that she understands Italian?

LOTTY. Try again, Mellersh.

MELLERSH. *Io … vo-gli-o … un … bag-no cal-do … Bag-no!* Bath! *(He mimes washing, drying.)* Bag-no! *(Costanza bursts out in laughter.)*

COSTANZA. *(Understanding.)* Ah! Il Signore vorrebbe un bagno caldo!

MELLERSH. Precisely. I think.

COSTANZA. *(Laughing, mimicking Mellersh's pronounciation and mime.)* Bag-no cal-do! Un momento, Signore. *("One moment." She exits into the villa, laughing.)* Santa Maria!

LOTTY. *(Applauding.)* Bravo! Bravo!

MELLERSH. *(Bowing playfully.)* Grat-zee, grat-zee. *(Sighs, smiles, looks around.)* This is a beautiful place, Charlotte.

LOTTY. Oh, I knew you'd like it!

MELLERSH. But I want to speak to you about the company you're keeping.

LOTTY. Well, I assure you, Mellersh ...

MELLERSH. Lady Caroline Bramble? Really, Charlotte.

LOTTY. Well, I ...

MELLERSH. You've been very clever, my dear!

LOTTY. Clever?

MELLERSH. I have planned precisely what I should say.

LOTTY. Oh, but you mustn't disturb Lady Caroline.

MELLERSH. I shall be the soul of discretion.

LOTTY. This isn't a business trip, Mellersh.

MELLERSH. No, but ...

LOTTY. Mellersh! *(Costanza enters with a towel and bath brush.)*

COSTANZA. *Bagno pronto, Signore. ("The bath is ready, sir.")*

LOTTY. I'll prepare your things. *(She gets his bag, leaves his hat.)*

MELLERSH. Thank you.

LOTTY. And be careful with the bath, Mellersh. It's very old. You mustn't turn the fire on until ...

MELLERSH. *(Impatiently.)* Thank you, Charlotte. *(Lotty exits. Mellersh starts for the villa, but Costanza blocks the entrance.)* Bag-no pron-to, you say?

COSTANZA. *Bagno pronto.*

MELLERSH. Very well, then. Thank you. *Grat-zee.*

COSTANZA. *Il bagno è molto vecchio e pericoloso, Signore. ("The bath is very old and dangerous, sir.")*

MELLERSH. *Pericoloso?*

COSTANZA. *(Nodding.) Sì. Bagno pericoloso. (Mellersh thinks, huffs, takes out his phrase book, thumbs through it. Costanza rolls her eyes, enunciates.) Pe — ri — co — lo ...*

MELLERSH. Yes, yes. *Pericoloso. (Finds it.)* Dangerous. Dangerous? A bath?

COSTANZA. *Sì. Bagno "booma!"*

MELLERSH. *Bag-no booma?* Good Heavens, I'm a big boy, thank you very much. I can surely take care of myself in a bath.

COSTANZA. *(Emphatically.) No, no! Bagno "booma," Signore! Deve stare molto attento! ("You must be very careful.")*

MELLERSH. Very well, *bag-no booma, bag-no booma. (He snatches the towel and brush.)* Now, shoo! Go on! *(Costanza scurries onto the terrace.) Grat-zee, Sig-norina. (He enters the villa.)*

COSTANZA. *(Curtsying sarcastically.) "Sig-norina!" (She huffs, bites her knuckle, clears the tea service, muttering. Lotty enters from*

*the villa, looking for Mellersh's hat.)*
LOTTY. *(Aglow.)* Oh, Costanza! *Paradiso,* Costanza. *Paradiso!*
COSTANZA. *(Humoring her.) Sì, sì,* Signora. *Paradiso! (Under her breath.) Inferno! ("Hell!") (Caroline enters from the villa, dressed for dinner, looking for Frederick.)*
LOTTY. Caroline! You are beautiful!
CAROLINE. Have you seen a man?
LOTTY. It's Mellersh! He's arrived!
CAROLINE. Oh, Lotty, good!
LOTTY. It's just as I saw it! But look here. Don't pay Mellersh any mind if he asks you a lot of questions.
CAROLINE. Questions?
LOTTY. With Mellersh, it's best to just say "marvelous," and leave it at that.
CAROLINE. I really am happy for you.
LOTTY. Thank you, Caroline! I can't wait for you to meet him! I am about to burst! *(There is an explosion from within the villa, followed by a pained wail. Clouds of steam pour forth. Mellersh runs out clad only in a small towel. The ladies stand, stunned, unnoticed.)*
MELLERSH. Damn that bath!
COSTANZA. *Bagno pericoloso! Bagno "booma!" (Mellersh spins, fumbles.)*
MELLERSH. *(To Costanza.)* Woman!
LOTTY. Mellersh! *(He spins.)*
MELLERSH. Charlotte!
LOTTY. This is most inappropriate, Mellersh.
MELLERSH. I could say as much!
CAROLINE. *(With great formality.)* I don't believe we've met.
MELLERSH. *(Spinning, aghast.)* Ah! Ha! No! No ... No, we haven't. I ... I'm afraid I used unpardonable language.
CAROLINE. *(Trying not to laugh.)* I thought it most appropriate. *(Lifting her hand, making the most of it.)* Lady Caroline Bramble.
MELLERSH. *(Smiling weakly at her hand.)* How do you do? *(Clears his throat, launches into what he had prepared, as if nothing were wrong.)* I had so been looking forward to our meeting. Mellersh Wilton, family soli ... *(He attempts to extend his hand, but the towel slips.)*
COSTANZA. Ah!
MELLERSH. Oh! *(Mrs. Graves enters from the villa.)*
MRS. GRAVES. *(Gasping, catching an eyeful.)* Oh!
MELLERSH. *(Surrounded.)* Good God!

58

CAROLINE. Mr. Wilton, may I introduce Mrs. Clayton Graves.

MRS. GRAVES. The pleasure is all mine!

LOTTY. Now you've met nearly everyone, Mellersh!

MELLERSH. How fortunate. *(To Mrs. Graves.)* How do you do? *(His towel slips again, exposing his backside. The ladies gasp, smiling. Costanza quicky covers Mellersh with his hat.)*

COSTANZA. *Signore. (He takes the hat.)*

MELLERSH. *Grat-zee. (He covers himself haphazardly with the hat and towel and inches toward the villa. The ladies can barely contain their laughter.)* Well ... well, this has been nice, but ... but you ... you ... you will ... perhaps another time would be ... *(With sudden formality, placing his hat on his head, bowing.)* Excuse me, ladies. *(He bolts into the villa. The ladies laugh. Wilding runs from the villa.)*

WILDING. Ladies, ladies. I am sorry. I should have tended to that heater immediately.

MRS. GRAVES. "In the flesh," indeed, Mrs. Wilton! *(Rose and Frederick run from the villa, straightening themselves.)*

ROSE. Lotty? What on earth?

LOTTY. Oh, it was only Mellersh, Rose.

CAROLINE. *(To Frederick.)* There you are! *(Frederick clutches Rose.)*

LOTTY. He's arrived!

WILDING. I suppose I had better make some introductions. Mrs. Graves, Mrs. Wilton, Lady Caroline, allow me to introduce Mrs. Arnott's ... *Mister* Arnott. *(Frederick smiles helplessly.)*

ROSE. Say hello, Frederick.

FREDERICK. *(Managing only a weak squeak.)* Hello!

MRS. GRAVES. *(Knowingly.)* You look flushed, my boy. One mustn't get too much sun too soon. Isn't that right, Lady Caroline? *(Caroline is frozen. She looks at Rose, who is beaming. She looks at Frederick.)*

CAROLINE. *(With complete grace.)* Yes, Mr. Arnott. We must find you a hat. *(The sound of piano music, Albéniz's "Suite Española No. 1 — Granada." Lights down.)*

## Scene 4

*Lights up on the terrace, later that evening. Deep blue moon-light. Caroline stands looking out into the garden. Music floats from the villa. Lotty enters from the villa, dressed for dinner.*

LOTTY. There you are. We're having a lovely time inside. What's the matter, Caroline? *(Caroline gathers herself.)*
CAROLINE. *(Lost.)* I was looking for ghosts. *(Lotty thinks, looks out.)*
LOTTY. They're everywhere, aren't they.
CAROLINE. Yes.
LOTTY. Mr. Wilding was asking after you.
CAROLINE. Mr. Wilding is very charming. As is your Mr. Wilton.
LOTTY. Thank you, Caroline. I should have never gotten him started on that piano, though.
CAROLINE. He plays beautifully.
LOTTY. He does, doesn't he!
CAROLINE. Did you see the full moon?
LOTTY. Somehow everything seems full tonight.
CAROLINE. It's love.
LOTTY. I suppose it is.
CAROLINE. The whole place reeks of it. I'll be leaving tomorrow, Lotty.
LOTTY. No, Caroline. *(Rose enters from the villa, dressed for dinner.)*
ROSE. Ladies, there's coffee if you'd like. Oh! A full moon! Beautiful!
CAROLINE. *(Warming.)* It must be great comfort to be so adored, Mrs. Arnott.
ROSE. Oh?
CAROLINE. You and your husband have been making eyes all evening.
ROSE. *(Glowing.)* We have, haven't we? It's been so long since Frederick has read his poetry.
LOTTY. It's wonderful, Rose.
ROSE. Even Mrs. Graves thought so!
CAROLINE. *(Genuinely.)* I really am so happy for you, Rose.

LOTTY. Caroline is lonely, Rose.

CAROLINE. Lotty!

LOTTY. I hadn't seen it until now, but look. *(Rose looks.)*

ROSE. We were sisters all along then, Caroline. *(Frederick enters from the villa, dressed for dinner.)*

FREDERICK. Is the party moving out here now?

LOTTY. Just admiring the view, Mr. Arnott.

FREDERICK. Ah!

ROSE. I'm surprised Mrs. Graves let you away.

LOTTY. Your poetry is lovely.

FREDERICK. Really?

LOTTY. Yes.

FREDERICK. No.

ROSE. *(Going to him.)* Don't be modest, Frederick.

FREDERICK. It's wonderful to see you like this, Rose.

ROSE. You as well. *(They kiss.)*

CAROLINE. You are a very lucky man, "Mr. Arnott."

FREDERICK. *(Sighs, smiles.)* I certainly am, "Lady Caroline." Thank you.

CAROLINE. Rose, you should show your husband the lower garden. In the moonlight it will be extraordinary.

LOTTY. Yes!

ROSE. Would you like to, Frederick?

FREDERICK. Very much.

ROSE. Very well. *(They walk toward the garden, stop.)* Lotty, tomorrow you must take Caroline boating.

LOTTY. Well, of course!

CAROLINE. No, I don't think ...

ROSE. You'll like that, Caroline. I see it! *(The ladies smile. Rose salutes.)* All'Italia!

LOTTY. All'Italia, Rose!

CAROLINE. All'Italia! *(Rose and Frederick exit into the garden. Lotty and Caroline watch after them, then look out.)* Is this really an enchanted place, Lotty?

LOTTY. Perhaps. You'll have to stay and find out. *(The piano has stopped, followed by soft applause and laughter from within the villa. Mrs. Graves enters from the villa arm-in-arm with Mellersh and Wilding. They are dressed for dinner and carry filled digestif glasses.)*

MRS. GRAVES. Well, I'm not sure London would be ready for Costanza's steak and kidney pie, but for a first effort I thought it exceptional. *(She sees Lotty and Caroline.)* Look, gentlemen. Sirens!

MELLERSH. You know, you might find this a bit fantastic, but the one bears a striking resemblance to my wife! *(Lotty smiles coyly.)*
LOTTY. Mellersh! *(Mellersh goes to her.)*
WILDING. *(Staying with Mrs. Graves.)* Lady Caroline. We've hardly heard a word from you all night. You aren't feeling ill again, I hope.
CAROLINE. Only thinking.
MRS. GRAVES. Lady Caroline is fond of thinking, Mr. Wilding.
CAROLINE. I was thinking what a wonderful host you've been, Mr. Wilding.
LOTTY. Yes.
MELLERSH. We should have proposed a toast to you at dinner.
MRS. GRAVES. *(To Wilding.)* Is there nothing that will convince you to stay with us a while longer?
WILDING. But I've already packed my things, so that Mr. Wilton may have the spare room tonight.
MELLERSH. The spare room?
LOTTY. Oh … oh, no, Mr. Wilding. Mr. Wilton shall share my room, of course.
WILDING. Well, then, I would be honored.
MELLERSH. *(Under his breath.)* The spare room, Charlotte?
LOTTY. What of Kate Lumley, Mrs. Graves? Have you written?
MRS. GRAVES. Kate Lumley? Oh, no, no. What Kate Lumley would make of macaroni alone I can but wonder. *(Thinks.)* Mr. Wilding, have you told Lady Caroline the story of the acacia?
WILDING. Well, no.
LOTTY. It's a lovely story, Caroline.
MRS. GRAVES. Perhaps you could show her the tree itself.
WILDING. I would like that very much. *(Caroline smiles.)*
CAROLINE. As would I.
WILDING. Well, right then. I'll get your stick, Mrs. Graves.
MRS. GRAVES. No, no. I've been without my stick all night. I'm not even sure where I left it. Go on now.
WILDING. Very well. *(Goes to Caroline.)* I'm afraid I've been remiss in my duties as host, Lady Caroline. I've been here two days now and I scarcely know a thing about you.
CAROLINE. You must not read the newspapers, Mr. Wilding.
WILDING. No. I don't.
CAROLINE. Well, you should. *(She looks at Lotty.)* You never know what you'll find. *(Wilding and Caroline exit into the garden. Mrs. Graves watches after them proudly.)*
MRS. GRAVES. There. That's better.

LOTTY. Mrs. Graves, perhaps you would read to us from the works of some of your great friends.

MELLERSH. Yes.

MRS. GRAVES. Somehow I'm not interested in hearing from my great friends tonight. They always say the same things, don't they?

MELLERSH. But surely their wisdom ...

LOTTY. And beauty ...

MRS. GRAVES. Yes. Yes. They are. Wise and beautiful. And it would be great folly to ever forget them. But they have one disadvantage. They're dead. If nothing else, at least we all do share the luxury of promise. *(Costanza enters from the villa, dressed in Mrs. Graves' costume from Act Two, Scene One, including hat. She carries a bowl of shelled nuts.)*

COSTANZA. *(Regally.)* "Thee nuts."

LOTTY. Costanza!

MELLERSH. *Meravigliosa! (Costanza bursts out in embarrassed giggles, regains her composure. Mrs. Graves goes to her.)*

MRS. GRAVES. Getting her into these things of mine was like getting a cat into a sack. And she's shelled the nuts! Took all the fun out of it. Mr. Wilton, could I charm you to the piano once more before I retire?

MELLERSH. Nothing would please me more.

MRS. GRAVES. I shall be waiting, then. *(Starts to exit into the villa, stops.)* Oh, and both of you please be prompt for breakfa ... *(Costanza raises her hand.)*

COSTANZA. Eh!

MRS. GRAVES. *(Begrudgingly.)* ... for *"colazione."*

COSTANZA. *(Proudly, to Lotty and Mellersh.)* Marvelous! *(Mrs. Graves and Costanza exit. A quiet moment.)*

LOTTY. What an enchanted night, Mellersh.

MELLERSH. It has indeed been quite nice, my dear. Have you been to our room this evening?

LOTTY. Not since dinner. Why?

MELLERSH. Someone has decorated it from floor to ceiling with flowers.

LOTTY. Really?

MELLERSH. Gave me quite a fright. *(Lotty smiles, looks out into the garden.)*

LOTTY. Mellersh! Look!

MELLERSH. *(Looking out.)* What?

LOTTY. There! The Roses are lovemaking.

MELLERSH. The "Roses"?

LOTTY. The Arnotts. Is Mrs. Arnott familiar to you, Mellersh?

MELLERSH. Mrs. Arnott? No.

LOTTY. From church. She's our disappointed Madonna.

MELLERSH. Is she? Well, fancy. I don't recall her being so attractive.

LOTTY. She's bloomed again. And there go the Carolines!

MELLERSH. Really, Charlotte.

LOTTY. Very well, Mellersh. The Wildings, then. And I'd wager we'll find Mrs. Graves' stick planted somewhere in the garden.

MELLERSH. Planted?

LOTTY. I'm sorry, Mellersh, but I see it. *(Mellersh opens his mouth to object. Lotty raises her hand confidently.)* Case closed, Mellersh.

MELLERSH. *(Softly.)* I thought I'd lost you, my dear.

LOTTY. Sometimes one just has to step back a bit. Your words, Mellersh.

MELLERSH. *(Surprised, pleasantly.)* Really?

LOTTY. *(In full glory.)* It's just a shame this all has to end. What could possibly follow such an enchanted April?

MELLERSH. I should think ... an enchanted May! *(Lotty beams, turns and kisses him fully. They are silent for a moment. Softly.)* I should go see to Mrs. Graves. *(He kisses Lotty, starts to exit, stops.)* Come in soon. *(He smiles and exits into the villa. Lotty looks after him, hugs herself, takes it all in. Albéniz's "Suite Española No. 1 — Granada" resumes. Finally, to us, completely enchanted.)*

LOTTY. "To those who appreciate wisteria and sunshine ... " *(Sighs.)* Not long after that evening, the wisteria at *San Salvatore* gave way, and, though a loss, the castle now dressed itself in triumphant white. There were white stocks and white pinks and white banksia roses, syringa and jessamine, and above all, the crowning glory of Mr. Wilding's acacia. A season had passed, and would pass again. And what I see now is that, enchantment aside, what had really been handed down that month was ... *(Sincerely.)* ... a lesson in gardening. The wisteria would return the following April. We all would, in fact. And there would be a wedding, and a new child. And Kate Lumley. But that first April we had only just planted our futures. And on our final day, as we reached the bottom of the hill and passed through the castle's gates, a great warm wind blew through and against our backs, as if to blow away our befores forever, now that our afters had begun. And with the wind came all the scents of *San Salvatore* ... the gardens and the sea, cinnamon and macaroni. And dancing among them, white blossoms! Breaking free! *(White petals start to fall. Lotty looks up, beaming, raises her arms skyward.)* Falling ... like rain! *(The lights fade as Lotty reaches higher through the falling petals.)*

## End of Play

# PROPERTY LIST

Towels
White petals
London *Times* (ROSE, LOTTY, CAROLINE)
Scissors, mirror, towel (MELLERSH)
Monocle (MELLERSH)
Book and pen (FREDERICK)
Gloves (LOTTY)
Bowl of nuts, nutcracker (MRS. GRAVES)
Photographs, postcard (WILDING)
Envelope (LOTTY)
Tea service (WILDING)
Dessert, napkin (MELLERSH)
Billfold with money (FREDERICK)
Italian phrase book (ROSE)
Travel bags (ROSE and LOTTY)
Beans, bowl (COSTANZA)
Book (CAROLINE)
Pitcher (MRS. GRAVES)
Bell (MRS. GRAVES)
Cards (MRS. GRAVES)
Pillow (CAROLINE)
Tea tray, bowl of nuts (COSTANZA)
Parasols (MRS. GRAVES, ROSE)
Flowers (LOTTY)
Flask (CAROLINE)
Bottle of castor oil (MRS. GRAVES)
Telegram (COSTANZA, LOTTY)
Bag of nuts (WILDING)
Canvas and easel (WILDING)
Tea tray with biscuits (COSTANZA)
Packages (LOTTY and MRS. GRAVES)
Card (COSTANZA)
Travel bag, hat, coat, phrase book (MELLERSH)
Towel (MELLERSH)
Filled digestif glasses (MELLERSH, WILDING, MRS. GRAVES)
Bowl of shelled nuts (COSTANZA)

# SOUND EFFECTS

Thunder
Rain
Train whistle
Train in motion
Church bell
Bell
Explosion
Albéniz's "Suite Española No. 1 — Granada"

# NEW PLAYS

★ **YELLOW FACE by David Henry Hwang.** Asian-American playwright DHH leads a protest against the casting of Jonathan Pryce as the Eurasian pimp in the original Broadway production of *Miss Saigon*, condemning the practice as "yellowface." The lines between truth and fiction blur with hilarious and moving results in this unreliable memoir. "A pungent play of ideas with a big heart." *–Variety.* "Fabulously inventive." *–The New Yorker.* [5M, 2W] ISBN: 978-0-8222-2301-6

★ **33 VARIATIONS by Moisés Kaufmann.** A mother coming to terms with her daughter. A composer coming to terms with his genius. And, even though they're separated by 200 years, these two people share an obsession that might, even just for a moment, make time stand still. "A compellingly original and thoroughly watchable play for today." *–Talkin' Broadway.* [4M, 4W] ISBN: 978-0-8222-2392-4

★ **BOOM by Peter Sinn Nachtrieb.** A grad student's online personal ad lures a mysterious journalism student to his subterranean research lab. But when a major catastrophic event strikes the planet, their date takes on evolutionary significance and the fate of humanity hangs in the balance. "Darkly funny dialogue." *–NY Times.* "Literate, coarse, thoughtful, sweet, scabrously inappropriate." *–Washington City Paper.* [1M, 2W] ISBN: 978-0-8222-2370-2

★ **LOVE, LOSS AND WHAT I WORE by Nora Ephron and Delia Ephron, based on the book by Ilene Beckerman.** A play of monologues and ensemble pieces about women, clothes and memory covering all the important subjects—mothers, prom dresses, mothers, buying bras, mothers, hating purses and why we only wear black. "Funny, compelling." *–NY Times.* "So funny and so powerful." *–WowOwow.com.* [5W] ISBN: 978-0-8222-2355-9

★ **CIRCLE MIRROR TRANSFORMATION by Annie Baker.** When four lost New Englanders enrolled in Marty's community center drama class experiment with harmless games, hearts are quietly torn apart, and tiny wars of epic proportions are waged and won. "Absorbing, unblinking and sharply funny." *–NY Times.* [2M, 3W] ISBN: 978-0-8222-2445-7

★ **BROKE-OLOGY by Nathan Louis Jackson.** The King family has weathered the hardships of life and survived with their love for each other intact. But when two brothers are called home to take care of their father, they find themselves strangely at odds. "Engaging dialogue." *–TheaterMania.com.* "Assured, bighearted." *–Time Out.* [3M, 1W] ISBN: 978-0-8222-2428-0

**DRAMATISTS PLAY SERVICE, INC.**
440 Park Avenue South, New York, NY 10016  212-683-8960  Fax 212-213-1539
postmaster@dramatists.com  www.dramatists.com

# NEW PLAYS

★ **A CIVIL WAR CHRISTMAS: AN AMERICAN MUSICAL CELEBRATION by Paula Vogel, music by Daryl Waters.** It's 1864, and Washington, D.C. is settling down to the coldest Christmas Eve in years. Intertwining many lives, this musical shows us that the gladness of one's heart is the best gift of all. "Boldly inventive theater, warm and affecting." –*Talkin' Broadway.* "Crisp strokes of dialogue." –*NY Times.* [12M, 5W] ISBN: 978-0-8222-2361-0

★ **SPEECH & DEBATE by Stephen Karam.** Three teenage misfits in Salem, Oregon discover they are linked by a sex scandal that's rocked their town. "Savvy comedy." –*Variety.* "Hilarious, cliché-free, and immensely entertaining." –*NY Times.* "A strong, rangy play." –*NY Newsday.* [2M, 2W] ISBN: 978-0-8222-2286-6

★ **DIVIDING THE ESTATE by Horton Foote.** Matriarch Stella Gordon is determined not to divide her 100-year-old Texas estate, despite her family's declining wealth and the looming financial crisis. But her three children have another plan. "Goes for laughs and succeeds." –*NY Daily News.* "The theatrical equivalent of a page-turner." –*Bloomberg.com.* [4M, 9W] ISBN: 978-0-8222-2398-6

★ **WHY TORTURE IS WRONG, AND THE PEOPLE WHO LOVE THEM by Christopher Durang.** Christopher Durang turns political humor upside down with this raucous and provocative satire about America's growing homeland "insecurity." "A smashing new play." –*NY Observer.* "You may laugh yourself silly." –*Bloomberg News.* [4M, 3W] ISBN: 978-0-8222-2401-3

★ **FIFTY WORDS by Michael Weller.** While their nine-year-old son is away for the night on his first sleepover, Adam and Jan have an evening alone together, beginning a suspenseful nightlong roller-coaster ride of revelation, rancor, passion and humor. "Mr. Weller is a bold and productive dramatist." –*NY Times.* [1M, 1W] ISBN: 978-0-8222-2348-1

★ **BECKY'S NEW CAR by Steven Dietz.** Becky Foster is caught in middle age, middle management and in a middling marriage—with no prospects for change on the horizon. Then one night a socially inept and grief-struck millionaire stumbles into the car dealership where Becky works. "Gently and consistently funny." –*Variety.* "Perfect blend of hilarious comedy and substantial weight." –*Broadway Hour.* [4M, 3W] ISBN: 978-0-8222-2393-1

**DRAMATISTS PLAY SERVICE, INC.**
440 Park Avenue South, New York, NY 10016  212-683-8960  Fax 212-213-1539
postmaster@dramatists.com  www.dramatists.com

# NEW PLAYS

★ **AT HOME AT THE ZOO by Edward Albee.** Edward Albee delves deeper into his play THE ZOO STORY by adding a first act, HOMELIFE, which precedes Peter's fateful meeting with Jerry on a park bench in Central Park. "An essential and heartening experience." *–NY Times.* "Darkly comic and thrilling." *–Time Out.* "Genuinely fascinating." *–Journal News.* [2M, 1W] ISBN: 978-0-8222-2317-7

★ **PASSING STRANGE book and lyrics by Stew, music by Stew and Heidi Rodewald, created in collaboration with Annie Dorsen.** A daring musical about a young bohemian that takes you from black middle-class America to Amsterdam, Berlin and beyond on a journey towards personal and artistic authenticity. "Fresh, exuberant, bracingly inventive, bitingly funny, and full of heart." *–NY Times.* "The freshest musical in town!" *–Wall Street Journal.* "Excellent songs and a vulnerable heart." *–Variety.* [4M, 3W] ISBN: 978-0-8222-2400-6

★ **REASONS TO BE PRETTY by Neil LaBute.** Greg really, truly adores his girlfriend, Steph. Unfortunately, he also thinks she has a few physical imperfections, and when he mentions them, all hell breaks loose. "Tight, tense and emotionally true." *–Time Magazine.* "Lively and compulsively watchable." *–The Record.* [2M, 2W] ISBN: 978-0-8222-2394-8

★ **OPUS by Michael Hollinger.** With only a few days to rehearse a grueling Beethoven masterpiece, a world-class string quartet struggles to prepare their highest-profile performance ever—a televised ceremony at the White House. "Intimate, intense and profoundly moving." *–Time Out.* "Worthy of scores of bravissimos." *–BroadwayWorld.com.* [4M, 1W] ISBN: 978-0-8222-2363-4

★ **BECKY SHAW by Gina Gionfriddo.** When an evening calculated to bring happiness takes a dark turn, crisis and comedy ensue in this wickedly funny play that asks what we owe the people we love and the strangers who land on our doorstep. "As engrossing as it is ferociously funny." *–NY Times.* "Gionfriddo is some kind of genius." *–Variety.* [2M, 3W] ISBN: 978-0-8222-2402-0

★ **KICKING A DEAD HORSE by Sam Shepard.** Hobart Struther's horse has just dropped dead. In an eighty-minute monologue, he discusses what path brought him here in the first place, the fate of his marriage, his career, politics and eventually the nature of the universe. "Deeply instinctual and intuitive." *–NY Times.* "The brilliance is in the infinite reverberations Shepard extracts from his simple metaphor." *–TheaterMania.* [1M, 1W] ISBN: 978-0-8222-2336-8

**DRAMATISTS PLAY SERVICE, INC.**
440 Park Avenue South, New York, NY 10016  212-683-8960  Fax 212-213-1539
postmaster@dramatists.com  www.dramatists.com

# NEW PLAYS

★ **AUGUST: OSAGE COUNTY by Tracy Letts.** WINNER OF THE 2008 PULITZER PRIZE AND TONY AWARD. When the large Weston family reunites after Dad disappears, their Oklahoma homestead explodes in a maelstrom of repressed truths and unsettling secrets. "Fiercely funny and bitingly sad." –*NY Times.* "Ferociously entertaining." –*Variety.* "A hugely ambitious, highly combustible saga." –*NY Daily News.* [6M, 7W] ISBN: 978-0-8222-2300-9

★ **RUINED by Lynn Nottage.** WINNER OF THE 2009 PULITZER PRIZE. Set in a small mining town in Democratic Republic of Congo, RUINED is a haunting, probing work about the resilience of the human spirit during times of war. "A full-immersion drama of shocking complexity and moral ambiguity." –*Variety.* "Sincere, passionate, courageous." –*Chicago Tribune.* [8M, 4W] ISBN: 978-0-8222-2390-0

★ **GOD OF CARNAGE by Yasmina Reza, translated by Christopher Hampton.** WINNER OF THE 2009 TONY AWARD. A playground altercation between boys brings together their Brooklyn parents, leaving the couples in tatters as the rum flows and tensions explode. "Satisfyingly primitive entertainment." –*NY Times.* "Elegant, acerbic, entertainingly fueled on pure bile." –*Variety.* [2M, 2W] ISBN: 978-0-8222-2399-3

★ **THE SEAFARER by Conor McPherson.** Sharky has returned to Dublin to look after his irascible, aging brother. Old drinking buddies Ivan and Nicky are holed up at the house too, hoping to play some cards. But with the arrival of a stranger from the distant past, the stakes are raised ever higher. "Dark and enthralling Christmas fable." –*NY Times.* "A timeless classic." –*Hollywood Reporter.* [5M] ISBN: 978-0-8222-2284-2

★ **THE NEW CENTURY by Paul Rudnick.** When the playwright is Paul Rudnick, expectations are geared for a play both hilarious and smart, and this provocative and outrageous comedy is no exception. "The one-liners fly like rockets." –*NY Times.* "The funniest playwright around." –*Journal News.* [2M, 3W] ISBN: 978-0-8222-2315-3

★ **SHIPWRECKED! AN ENTERTAINMENT—THE AMAZING ADVENTURES OF LOUIS DE ROUGEMONT (AS TOLD BY HIMSELF) by Donald Margulies.** The amazing story of bravery, survival and celebrity that left nineteenth-century England spellbound. Dare to be whisked away. "A deft, literate narrative." –*LA Times.* "Springs to life like a theatrical pop-up book." –*NY Times.* [2M, 1W] ISBN: 978-0-8222-2341-2

**DRAMATISTS PLAY SERVICE, INC.**
440 Park Avenue South, New York, NY 10016  212-683-8960  Fax 212-213-1539
postmaster@dramatists.com   www.dramatists.com